Integrative Advisory Services

Expanding Your Accounting Services Beyond the Cloud

Amy Vetter, CPA, CITP, CGMA

WILEY

For general information on our other products and services or for technical support, please contact our Customer Care Department within the United States at (800) 762-2974, outside the United States at (317) 572-3993, or fax (317) 572-4002.

Wiley publishes in a variety of print and electronic formats and by print-on-demand. Some material included with standard print versions of this book may not be included in e-books or in print-on-demand. If this book refers to media such as a CD or DVD that is not included in the version you purchased, you may download this material at http://booksupport.wiley.com. For more information about Wiley products, visit www.wiley.com.

Library of Congress Cataloging-in-Publication Data is Available:

ISBN 9781119415978 (Hardcover)
ISBN 9781119422006 (ePDF)
ISBN 9781119422020 (ePub)

Cover Design: Wiley
Cover Image: © Jorg Greuel/Getty Images

Printed in the United States of America.
10 9 8 7 6 5 4 3 2 1

Contents

Preface

Integrative Advisory Services is the CPA, accounting professional, and bookkeeper's guide to the future. As technology paves the way for increased self-reliance and do-it-yourself financial services, much of the traditional data entry tasks of accounting professionals and bookkeepers will be reduced. It is time for the accounting industry to change how it does business.

Nothing can replace the human side of the client–advisor experience and the desire to improve clients' businesses with financial information. Technology will continue to march forward, so accounting professionals must adapt to the changing marketplace to thrive in this new paradigm.

This book shows how to provide the kind of value that technology cannot offer: human connection. Rather than simply reporting data, today's accounting professionals have an opportunity to take a more active role in their clients' business by analyzing the story behind the numbers, understanding both operations and finance, and guiding their clients toward the outcomes they need.

Learn how to take on more of an advisory role and become a critical component of your clients' success by:

- Spending less time crunching numbers and more time advising clients
- Becoming an integral part of your clients' decision-making process
- Providing real value by communicating financial data analysis
- Becoming the strategic partner your client cannot do without—a cherished advisor

Acknowledgments

I want to thank my husband, Rob, and my children, Jagger and Austin, who have supported me through the ups and downs of my career and encouraged me to always strive for what my heart desires.

My grandfather has been a mere memory since I was 3 years old at the time of his passing, but he had a huge impact on my career. His legacy inspired me to pursue a life's mission of helping small businesses survive and grow.

My mother provided the example of being a business owner herself and involved me at a young age. She provided me with the experience that created the foundation and vision of what I wanted to do with my life.

A heartfelt thanks to my clients over the years, who taught me so much about the right and wrong ways to advise them. The experience I gained from seeing the impact of my advice on their businesses was so satisfying and rewarding that I have made a career since of training others on how to do it as well.

Much gratitude to Xero Accounting Software, who provided the support and encouragement for me to put this book together.

For their time and expertise, I want to thank Kathryn Duggan, Alex Mercer, Himanshu Singh, Matthew Solan, and Corina Standiford. Your contributions to this process of writing of this book have made a great impact.

I also want to thank the accounting practices from around the world that contributed real-world examples from their firms that supplement the topics described in this book: Amanda Aguillard, Aaron Berson, Paul Bulpitt, David Emmerman, Will Farnell, Jay Kimelman, Kenji Kuramoto, Shelly Lingor, Michael Lopez, Ryan Miller, Neil Sinclair, James Solomons, and Ryan Watson. Their contributions show not only the universal struggles of accountants, but also how we can overcome them by being innovative (and smart) about the need to create long-lasting and prosperous relationships with our clients. Their expert insight is much appreciated.

Additional thanks to Sheck Cho, Michael Henton, Judy Howarth, and Alex Vegbey at Wiley for their support and answers throughout the process.

Introduction

Since I was 12 years old, I knew I was going to be a certified public accountant (CPA). I grew up with stories about my Grandfather's CPA practice, which he began in the 1930s with the purpose of positively impacting the business owners in his immigrant neighborhood in St Paul, Minnesota. He was what I call the *cherished advisor* of his day—providing guidance to small business owners on financial decisions that were strategic for their businesses. Their relationships went way beyond figures and numbers.

My mother, as she grew up, decided not to become an accountant and instead was drawn toward the arts. However, her natural business acumen ended up coming out later when she opened her own maid service operation when I was young. I was involved right from the beginning. After school, I often worked the front desk and did various administrative tasks. I learned early on about the importance of knowing your numbers as a business owner because, unfortunately, my mom was not an accountant, and she found herself making decisions that ended up being detrimental to her business in the long run.

Like many small business owners at the time, my mom didn't have an accountant who was an advisor. Instead, due to limitations of technology, she received strictly compliance financials, and many times six to nine months after the financial year was over. She had no insight into the numbers, nor an accountant who could explain her performance, so she was left to make financial decisions without any guidance.

When my mom took me to trade shows and conferences for her business, I would ask other business owners what major I should choose when entering college. The answer was unanimous: accounting. They told me that no matter what career I eventually chose, having an accounting background would help me make better decisions in business.

In hindsight, I wonder about the root cause of this statement. Is it necessary for everyone to have an accounting degree to run a business? The answer should be no, because if you have an accountant involved with a business who provides insight and advice, the business owner should be able to stay focused on what they are good at, leaving the financial analysis to the experts. But my guess was that these business owners were not getting the advice and involvement from their accountants they needed.

Fast forward to today. We have finally reached a pinnacle moment in the accounting industry in which cloud technology, as well as the onset of artificial intelligence and machine learning, has greatly reduced the time and effort needed for traditional data entry and number crunching.

Technology provides us the opportunity to take our practices in a new and rewarding direction. We can now restructure our firms to offer services to clients that they have wanted for years. There are no more excuses as to why we can't offer these services—only ourselves and not taking the time to restructure our practices. Our clients are adopting the most up-to-date technology on a regular basis. In turn, as accounting professionals, we need to keep up with their needs and be familiar with how they conduct their business and interact with customers.

This new direction for accounting is not a trend. It is the future. The rapid pace of change is one we have never seen before in our industry. Now is the time to make an investment not only in your professional future, but also that of your business.

I have worked with accounting practices and small businesses for more than 20 years as an accountant, advisor, and consultant—offering advice and guidance on how to make these changes in an organized and effective fashion. I have gathered all my experience and interactions over the years into this book to create a comprehensive plan that guides you through building an integrative advisory service for your practice.

The approach goes beyond the latest technology. It's about creating the soft skills needed to market, sell, and deliver your advisory services. It's about how to create the necessary change management and quality control procedures needed internally to ensure you offer only the best service to your clients. It's about learning the skills to guide conversations with a client that go beyond the accounting, to give them the advice they need to maintain positive cash flow, to prevent them from making bad purchasing decisions, or to find innovative ways to create more efficient overhead to generate more profitability.

By becoming a cherished advisor, you will learn how to create an experience for your clients that they have not had before with other accountants or bookkeepers. You become an integral part of the real-time decision-making process; services are delivered proactively, rather than reactively; and you understand both the operational and financial sides of the business. As a result, you become a strategic partner that the business appreciates, highly values, and cherishes.

This book provides the steps you need for this journey into the next phase of accounting. Rather than worrying about whether your job will one day be replaced, be proactive and learn how to retool your skills to be ahead of the pack. The culmination will be that you can integrate these advisory services into your practice, expand your services beyond cloud technology, and be cherished by your clients.

CHAPTER 1

History of the Accounting Profession

From Compliance to Advisory

You could say that accounting is literally in my blood. My grandfather's family immigrated to the United States from Russia in 1909. They lived in an immigrant neighborhood in Minnesota, a tightly knit community where everyone set their sights on a better life.

As immigrants, my family saw accounting as an attractive profession because it supplied a steady job. At the end of the day, every type of business needs help keeping their books.

My grandfather worked hard and became a Certified Public Accountant (CPA) in 1935, in the depths of the Depression, and early in the formation of the accounting profession in the United States. He worked as a CPA until 1977, when he passed away. Throughout his career, he experienced massive shifts in the accounting profession.

From the stories I have heard about my grandfather, he was not today's model of a CPA. He saw the business as not just a way to earn a good living to support his family, but as a way to help his community. He was a one-person operation. He cultivated clients by word of mouth. He had an office with some contractors and used the traditional paper ledger and sharp pencils.

Of course in his days—the Stone Age of accounting by today's standards—accounting was strictly pen and paper. The lone piece of technology was often a 10-key machine. The "cloud" was folders in filing cabinets, each carefully labeled and arranged. These were the polished wingtips and bow ties days of accounting.

What made his work as a CPA different from that of many of the CPAs of today is that back then, 100 percent of his business revolved around personal connections. As an immigrant himself, living through the Depression, he worked to help other small business owners thrive and achieve their goals of protecting their assets and families. The thinking was simple: If he helped the business grow then his practice would thrive in turn.

My grandfather was what I like to call a *cherished advisor*. He was not just an accountant in the traditional sense. His practice was about building partnerships with clients. What could he do to make their business better? He made a personal investment, and it paid off.

As I grew up, what I heard about my grandfather was that he got to know his clients—and they got to know him. He met with them on a regular basis and sat down with them to go over their financial reports. He listened. They asked questions. He offered advice and insight. They were a team, and they worked together.

I was also told about how he would trade services with his clients, such as receiving a new fur coat for my mom each year when she was a child, or season tickets to the symphony. As times were financially strained for most people, these arrangements built strength in the loyalty of his clients because he was part of their struggle and wanted to find ways to help.

My grandfather's generation had a unique perspective on the industry from its beginning. They experienced perhaps the greatest evolution of the accounting profession. It began with little regulation and expanded to an extreme ramp-up of tax codes and accounting principles for businesses and individuals. Organization practice evolved from manual paper filing to the development of innovative technology such as accounting software and the industry-changing cloud technology, enabling information to be filed away with a few mouse clicks.

TECHNOLOGY AND HUMANS

Yes, technology has been wonderful for our industry. With each improvement in software, it has aided all CPAs to complete our work faster. This ongoing evolution in our industry has never meant that there is less need for an accountant or a bookkeeper in business. Our generation now experiences the most profound advancements in cloud technology with machine learning, artificial intelligence, new economies, and alternative currencies.

Many fear that the traditional data entry tasks of accounting professionals and bookkeepers will be reduced, or even disappear. But it is actually the traditional tasks of accounting that we are meant to do. We should work toward getting back to the kind of client relationships our profession once cherished, like the relationships my grandfather experienced.

Due to the increase in compliance with regulations that were placed upon the industry over the decades, and technology not moving fast enough to help us, we may have lost something vital in the process: our advisory relationship with clients.

Instead of striving to improve our client's business with the financial information we provide, like my grandfather did, we have had to spend the majority of office hours trying to keep up with ever-increasing deadlines and extensions. Our only real connection with clients is when we present facts and figures via e-mail. Otherwise, we only sit down with them maybe once or twice a year, just like seeing our dentist.

When was the last time you met with clients? I mean really met with them. When did you sit down and discuss their goals, short- and long-term objectives, and where they need the most help and guidance?

The human side of accounting can never be replaced by technology—only enhanced. Accounting professionals now have an opportunity to create real value for their business-owner or CEO clients. The advances in technology can free up our time, which can now be devoted to more meaningful client conversations beyond just communicating the analysis of their financial data. This approach can change the dynamic and outcome of your CPA–client relationship. You can help your clients make informed decisions about cash flow, business forecasting, and financial strategy to help them succeed and thrive. In other words, you can become a cherished advisor.

As a cherished advisor, the accounting professional becomes an integral part of the real-time decision making process. The process becomes proactive—rather than reactive—as you better understand both the operational and financial sides of your client's business. As a result, you, the CPA, become a strategic partner that the business appreciates and highly values.

Now is the prime time to move forward into the next generation of accounting. And you can do this by looking backward.

By learning the lessons of how accounting used to operate, and taking advantage of the current and future generations of accounting professionals, you can create vertical industry niche practices in your accounting business from which you offer outsourced advisory services for specific industries—and build or grow your practice in ways that were never before possible. You can become a cherished advisor for this next generation of clients as your take your practice into the future.

LOOKING BACK ON ACCOUNTING

To understand where we need to go, we first have to look at where we came from. As the world changed how it conducted business, and as new countries were developed with expanding governments, the accounting industry slowly was bogged down in regulations, new tax laws, and financial oversight. Exploring the evolution of accounting can provide insight into where we may have gotten off the path of personal connection and how we can find our way back.

Have you ever heard of Luca Pacioli? He is often regarded as one of the founding fathers of accounting. In 1494, he first described the system of double-entry bookkeeping used by Venetian merchants in his book of mathematics, *Summa de Arithmetica, Geometria, Proportioni et Proportionalita* (*Summary of Arithmetic, Geometry, Proportions, and Proportionality*).

Businesses and governments had been recording financial information long before this, but it was Pacioli who was the first to describe the system of inputting debits and credits in ledgers, which is still the basis of today's accounting systems.

For the next 200-plus years, through the 1700s, both large and small innovations were added to the double-entry records approach. For example, the East India Company—the powerhouse trade company of the 18th century that linked the East Indies with Western Europe—strengthened the concept of invested capital and dividend distribution. As a result, they could attract more investors to fuel the enterprise through expansion and investment in stronger business practices. This approach also created the need for a change in financial accounting and managerial accounting. The first was how the company presented its financials to gain investors, and the second was used so that the business could be run as efficiently as possible.

In America, the first big change in accounting occurred in 1862, at the height of the Civil War. This is when President Abraham

Lincoln approved the creation of the Internal Revenue Service (now more commonly known as the IRS) and the nation's first income tax. The IRS was a revenue-raising measure to help pay for the war's expenses. The IRS levied a 3-percent tax on annual incomes between $600 and $10,000, and a 5-percent tax on income more than $10,000. The new taxes created a surge in accounting because everyone's income had to be recorded and reported to the IRS.

At the same time, the concept of business was changing. Originally, the concept of business was to do one thing at a time. Take the agriculture business, for example. A farmer would raise sheep for wool. The wool would be sold to a company who would make a sweater, or some other garment, whenever a customer requested one. The accounting transactions were linear. One input created another output, so the recording of those transactions were simpler in nature.

All that changed with the development of mass production and assembly-line technology of the Industrial Revolution throughout the 19th century. Businesses could create goods faster and more efficiently than they could by hand. It was a new, yet complex, way of doing business, with multiple inputs for work in progress, but it was successful. It helped to spur more consumer demand for cheaper products, which in turn stimulated the need for more production, and the entire commercial engine began to hum along.

Accounting grew alongside this new era of industry. More transactions and complexity created the need for more advanced cost-accounting systems, as well as a way to report these activities on financial statements.

As these new industries grew, larger corporations were created that desired more classes of external capital providers: shareowners and bondholders. These were individuals who were not part of the firm's management, but had a vital interest in its results. Accountants had to evolve how they did business and expand on the traditional double-entry accounting methods.

The rising public status of accountants helped to transform accounting into a powerful profession. In 1887, 31 accountants gathered in New York City to form the first accounting organization: the American Association of Public Accountants (AAPA). The title and professional license of the Certified Public Accountant (CPA) followed in 1896. The AAPA eventually became the American Institute of Accountants, which changed its name in 1957 to the current American Institute of Certified Public Accountants (AICPA) and now has more than 410,000 members in 143 countries.

Perhaps accounting's greatest challenges that paved the way to today's dilemma occurred during the depths of the Great Depression. After the stock market crash in 1929, the Securities and Exchange Commission (SEC) was formed in an effort to avoid another Wall Street meltdown. Henceforth, all publicly traded companies had to file periodic reports with the Commission to be certified by members of the accounting profession.

At the same time, filing individual taxes became more complex. The Congress passed the Revenue Act of 1942, which was hailed by President Franklin Roosevelt as "the greatest tax bill in American history." This act increased the number of Americans who were subject to income tax and the amount of those taxes, but it also created deductions for medical and investment expenses.

This was when the compliance era began to hit its stride. For the next several decades, the accounting profession felt the weight of stricter tax rules that made accounting standards denser and more complex. There were more forms to fill out; more laws to read, understand, and follow; and more deadlines.

When you think about this from a professional standpoint, what appears to have happened is that as compliance grew, accounting got more complicated and time intense. Accountants began to spend more time in siloed offices, buried in paperwork and deciphering government regulations, and less time fostering client relationships.

To put it into perspective, in 1935, the 1040 form included two pages of instructions; now it is well over 200 pages. The number of pages in the federal tax law has exploded from 400 pages in 1913 to more than 74,000 pages (and still growing) today.

You can see how an accountant's time shifted to dealing with paperwork, rather than meeting with clients on real-time questions they had about their businesses. Still, it was a slow transition, and the industry got comfortable with the new way in which it provided services. It began to focus more on crunching numbers, filling out forms, and abiding by ever-changing rules. Meanwhile, contacts with clients became more infrequent.

The result: Invisible walls began going up in accounting offices around the country. Accountants often worked alone and only interacted with clients when there was a need, which was typically about delivering compliance work.

Accountants who are too plugged into this compliance work become rusty when it comes to client interactions and offering sound advice. I have spoken to many business owners over the years who complain that their accountant does not call them back when they need advice about their business. When I speak with accountants, they say the reason for this is two fold: (1) they lack the time, and (2) they worry that the client may ask a question they don't know the answer to. For many accountants, they don't want to feel inadequate if they don't know the answer to a question at the precise moment a client asks a question, so they end up avoiding the interaction.

This is where the advancements in technology can help transform our profession. By using cloud technology to break down walls between accountants and clients instead of building new ones, we can get back to the cherished advisor status previously associated with a CPA, an accountant, or a bookkeeper.

As accountants, we can take this to a whole new level by allowing cloud technology to take care of the many compliance requirements, thus enabling us to spend more time with our clients to help them improve their businesses. That is when we can achieve the cherished advisor status, which is more than just providing necessary and accurate financial information—it's becoming an advisor whom a client cannot imagine living without. As a cherished advisor, you provide so much value that your clients consider the fee for your services as an investment in their business because they can get the advice they need when they need it, and they do not have to wait until tax time to get your attention.

This is what we need to return to—this is what our clients want. The technology of today and the future will allow us to get back out there and follow the footsteps of the accountants of my grandfather's generation and earlier.

Studies and surveys have found that there was a clear divide between what our clients wanted and what a business needed. There was also a divide within a company about what accountants deliver versus what they think accountants should deliver. Here are some highlights of recent research on this topic:

- In a 2014 survey conducted by The Sleeter Group, 85 percent of small businesses said they wanted their CPAs to be more proactive in technology.[1]
- According to a report by KPMG International, one in three CEOs don't think their CFO is providing the value they need.[2]
- According to a study conducted by EY in 2013, 66 percent of global CEOs do not think the title CFO accurately describes the role's diversity.[3]

This highlights an interesting divide between what we accountants value versus what our clients value. Traditionally, accountants have valued their services by the billable hour—our time is our inventory. However, when our clients and CEOs want information, they don't care how long it took to calculate—they just want the answers the numbers provide to help their business better perform. The quicker, the better. And technology, especially cloud technology, provides the speed to deliver results in real time. The gap is that those results are just numbers (also referred to as data). The value of a cherished advisor is the expertise to decipher what the numbers mean and how to make a positive impact on the business. The challenge is to change the mind-set of clients from "credence good" to "experience good" regarding what an accountant delivers to them. "Credence good" is the client saying, "I think I receive good value from my CPA. I don't know what they do, but I guess their fee is worth it."

In comparison, "experience good" is a client's familiarity with the accountant, when the client cannot imagine not having the accountant as a part of their business. They feel that you, as their accountant, are an integral part of their business and provide them with the advice they need when they need it. Clients like this understand the value of what a CPA, an accountant, or a bookkeeper provides. Accountants should make it their goal to become cherished advisors—not just instruments for producing financial data, but rather trusted counselors and partners to their clients.

REACHING FOR THE CLOUD

In essence, cloud technology has really just begun to take hold. The development began in the late 1990s and early 2000s, and it has been growing steadily ever since. But it was only recently that early adopters in the accounting profession and their clients began to understand its value.

What makes cloud technology such a game changer for the accounting profession is that it has radically altered how information arrives into the firm. Before this, financial information came into the accountant's office from various points and in different formats. The individual client didn't understand the desired end result—instead, he or she dumped a mountain of data onto the accountant's desk and did not really appreciate what it took to get all of it in proper order.

Of course, with much disarray in how financial information was provided—and the extra time needed to organize and manage it—the time frame for presenting financial reports took a while. As a result, it was common for clients not to receive reports up to six to nine months after their financial year ended, because extensions were needed. And often, by the time the client received the financial reporting, it was too late in the next year to make significant changes based on the results.

But with cloud technology, this manual work is no longer necessary. All the information that comes from banks, suppliers, and customers can now be directly fed into one system at one time. From there, it is much easier to interpret data, provide instant analysis, and deliver financial reports that can help clients make changes in their business in real time. With more control over the information, accountants have the opportunity to develop all kinds of analyses to help their clients succeed.

For instance, cloud accounting software programs have taken what was locked in several desktops and created a central place where data can feed in from multiple sources. This creates more of a platform than accounting software alone can provide. The actual accounting is just one piece of the platform. The other components are the various types of information received by the software from multiple data sources—such as banks, vendors, and clients.

From this single platform, we can step back and consolidate the information to take a broader look at a company's financial picture—as well as get close to study details that may be influencing daily business practices. It allows us to better analyze the data to figure out where things are going in the wrong direction and how we can improve.

The cloud also allows us to access information through mobile devices. When data is available on tablets, laptops, and smartphones, you can allow anyone to access that data anytime and anywhere. This accessibility helps to streamline the process and provide faster turnaround. It also allows an advisor to be more proactive and send alerts to clients about immediate actions that need to be taken.

As you can imagine, this new operational approach can begin to alter the entire relationship between the accountant and the client and create more value for the services we provide.

While this surge in technology may seem like a job-killer for accountants and bookkeepers since it replaces much of the work they had been doing, it is important to realize that in the past, technology has always replaced some tasks.

There is still great demand for more technical accountants—regulatory experts who can understand changes to Generally Accepted Accounting Principles (GAAP) and ensure that management and staff comply. But for the more mundane accounting tasks, many companies are turning to software, which leads to smaller staff sizes. For example, in 2015, North American Substation Services LLC searched for an accountant to collect, record, and reconcile payments. But in the end, they decided to install software instead of adding a person to the team. The reason for this decision was that the computer program could analyze data and help make the company's payments system more efficient with no thinking involved.[4]

This trend has rippled throughout the finance industry. According to the consulting firm Hackett Group, large financial companies reduced the number of jobs by almost 50 percent from 2002 to 2017.[5]

Smaller companies are also moving in this direction. For example, Yieldbot Inc., an online advertising company, has $45 million in revenue but only employs four people in its finance department. The company relies on software programs to perform and manage everyday accounting tasks like sending notices to customers, correcting errors in the financial statements, and making sure regulatory filing requirements are met. "It frees us up to make sure we can operate with the leanest possible headcount," Matthew Horn, director of finance, told the *Wall Street Journal*.[6]

Does that mean that accountants should fear this technology? No—just the opposite. They should welcome it as a way to discover all kinds of new opportunities, the main one being "re-tooling" to provide what software can never do—replicate human interaction.

HUMANITY VERSUS MACHINE

Ever since humans first created electronic technology, there has been an underlying fear that somehow, someday, technology would rise up to defeat us. Look at the early days of science fiction. The themes have always involved humanity's electronic creations turning on us. Stanley Kubrick's classic film *2001: A Space Odyssey* put this phobia squarely in our psyche when HAL 9000, the supercomputer, turns on the very scientific minds that created it.

This was 1968, just when computers were entering the workplace and changing not only how we worked, but in what capacity. Sure, technology can make businesses run more smoothly and more efficiently, but at what cost? What do we give up?

In the early decades of the 1900s, mathematical and technical calculations were done manually rather than by machine. This required a large workforce to compute all the information. With the industrial boom brought on by World War II, organizations like NASA began to recruit women for this work.

As computer technology began to develop and expand, many of these manual tasks were automated. However, rather than discard the women that had previously done this job, NASA and other organizations simply retrained employees to work alongside these new computers and perform less menial tasks.

This new attitude toward technology was beautifully showcased in the Oscar-award-winning film *Hidden Figures*. African-American physicist and mathematician Katherine Johnson and her team worked as "computers" on NASA's early team from 1953 to 1958, analyzing topics like gust alleviation for aircrafts.

During one pivotal scene in the film, a giant IBM computer is carted in, which stuns the collection of NASA workers. The initial reaction from many of the workers is one of fear and intimidation. They are afraid that this machine will replace them since machines can do things better, faster, and more efficiently than humans—and no doubt will end up costing less. But there were others who saw the introduction of supercomputers into their industry as an opportunity. This new phase opened up new careers in computer engineering, software development, and technical support. It created a wave of new jobs instead of only eliminating existing ones.

This has been the accounting industry's basic attitude to technology as well. Yes, some saw it as a job threat, but for the most part, the early adopters embraced how it could actually *improve* their work and thus increase their value to their clients. Businesses will still need accountants, but the definition of what clients will expect from their accountants is going to change.

Giant computers began to enter our profession, just like with NASA, and took up entire floors in the office. But these new machines could store and spit out data that used to take hours to go through. Over the years, computers got smaller while their capacities grew larger.

We actually took advantage of this change through the years. These machines ended up helping accountants to do more in less time. Instead of paper ledgers and manual calculations, we moved to designing spreadsheets in Microsoft Excel. Now cloud technology will allow us to go even further by speeding up profit and loss projections and budgeting and cash flow projections and providing clients with more in-depth financial information, so we can spend more time on the conversation than on calculating data.

NEW OPPORTUNITIES ABOUND

Here is something to think about: The current job description of an accounts payable (A/P) clerk will disappear in possibly 20 years. This may seem like a bleak prediction, but the reality is that software advances, developments in robotics, artificial intelligence, and machine learning are bringing a new age of automation—one in which machines will be able to outperform humans in various work tasks.

The McKinsey Global institute's January 2017 report on the future of automation, titled "A Future that Works: Automation, Employment, and Productivity," suggests that adapting current technology has the potential to automate about 50 percent of the world's current work activities.[7] The activities most susceptible to this automation are repetitive, noncreative tasks such as data collection and processing. This puts at risk many jobs in areas such as customer service, sales, invoicing, account management, and other data-entry positions.

However, these projections don't necessarily mean that the future is hopeless for those holding A/P positions. Skilled employees will continue to work alongside software automation and robotic-process automation to approve data analysis, guide software in the right direction, and even perform tasks that do not yet exist.

This change will require some new skills-based learning, but it is also an opportunity for A/P department employees to step out from behind the curtain and develop their job descriptions. It means employees will be able to focus on raising their profiles, supporting the business with more meaningful work, providing good internal service, and in turn, becoming more motivated.

I mention all of this because it provides an excellent example of the fertile ground available for accountants to become cherished advisors. The new generation of accountants often is looking for opportunities that a cherished advisor climate offers.

Take a look at this poll reported by the cloud accounting software company Xero. It asked accounting firms what services they offer their clients. Here is what it found:

- Compliance/tax: 48 percent
- Bookkeeping: 41 percent
- Strategic planning: 30 percent
- Accounting software consulting (implementation/add-on select): 21 percent

Nothing wrong with this, and you would probably expect the numbers to make sense. But look closer.

The smallest area—consulting—is the greatest area of new growth, yet the majority of accounting firms have not heavily invested in it. I believe one reason for this is that financial consultants are still entrenched in the traditional services that bring in revenue today. To make this change for the future, it is important to invest in the development of consulting and assign personnel to begin putting this potential new business line together.

WHERE DOES YOUR BUSINESS GO FROM HERE?

Why is this move to a cherished advisor so important to the future of the profession? Cloud technology has forever changed how accountants conduct business and what clients will come to expect from their accounting relationship. This also has the ability to attract a new generation of accountants who offer special skills to innovative firms. This can create a perfect storm for accounting firms to begin specializing in certain industries and become industry experts.

This shift also has the potential to prepare a company for the future in terms of succession planning and grooming future partners. Where do you want your company to go, and who should lead the way?

With today's cloud accounting platforms, you are able to offer services in new and innovative ways. Many of the typical accounting data-entry tasks are now automated, which allows you to be more creative in the accounting services you offer. Yet, many accounting students and young professionals are still unaware that accounting careers outside of tax and audit are available to them—and what these careers may offer. In this way, cloud technology is the best recruiting tool for this group as potential cherished advisors.

According to research from the Pew Research Center conducted in 2015, more than one in three workers today are in the "millennial" category—ages 18 to 34—and this group has surpassed the Baby Boomers in terms of number of labor force workers.[8]

What are millennials looking for in terms of potential employers and career choices? In a 2011 survey conducted by PwC, a global accounting and consulting firm, 59 percent of millennials said an employer's provision of technology is important to them, and 78 percent said using technology they like makes them more effective.[9] This group was also looking for the potential to grow in their field. In fact, the same survey found that what most attracted millennials when choosing a potential employer was an opportunity for career progression (see Figure 1.1).

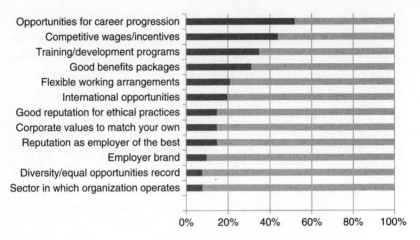

Figure 1.1 Millennials at Work: What Do They Look for in Potential Employers?
Source: *Millennials at Work: Reshaping the Workplace, PricewaterhouseCooper, 2011.*

According to the survey, millennials also are not interested in working 60-hour weeks doing redundant work. In terms of ideal work scenarios, the survey respondents mentioned things like mentorships, adherence to a specified mission, growth opportunities, room to learn, a collaborative culture, working together, work-life balance, and having a fun work environment.

The millennial generation is looking to move beyond traditional roles of accounting and billing for their time. They are searching for something more meaningful and personal from their career choices, and they are open to this new direction of building client relationships. After all, this is the generation of Facebook, Twitter, and Instagram. They are more accustomed to sharing and connecting with people through technology.

Sound familiar? This is what my grandfather had actually created in his CPA practice of long ago: the integration between work and life, and the common thread that tied his purpose to the work that he did with his clients.

Of course, change management of this level can be a challenge. You can have the best intentions, but without a well-thought-out strategy, the proper resources, and the time and dedication to commit to it, your efforts will ultimately fail. The next chapter discusses in more detail what kind of investment you need to make to create a cherished advisor platform for you and your business. But keep in mind that accountant–client relationships are just like personal relationships. You need to put in the time, effort, and attention to make them work.

Becoming a cherished advisor is about creating the next phase of services you can offer as an accounting and bookkeeping professional. The human side of the experience will never be replaced by technology, only enhanced. You have the unique opportunity to learn the skills to become an advisor, help develop advisors for your business, and create and maintain ongoing relationships with your clients throughout the year.

As a cherished advisor, you will become an integral part of the real-time decision-making process, be proactive (rather than reactive), and understand both the operational and financial sides of the business. As a result, you will become a strategic partner that your clients will highly value. With proper planning and by following the necessary steps explained throughout this book, you can create and offer these valuable services in the future.

SUMMARY

Accountants of the early 20th century focused their practice on developing strong client–accountant relationships, and businesses valued CPAs as trusted advisors to help improve their bottom lines. However, the addition of new tax laws and regulations increased the workload of CPAs, and more time was devoted to managing compliancy issues. As a result, client–accountant relationships began to wane. This chapter explored the evolution of accounting technology through the decades, including today's cloud technology, which has enabled CPAs, accountants, and bookkeepers to do more work, more efficiently. While this dramatic switch has many in the accounting industry worried about future employment, it also invites an opportunity for CPAs to build new client–accountant relationships and once again become cherished advisors. This can help identify and develop niches for new business growth.

ENDNOTES

1. Isaac M. O'Bannon, "What Do Small Business Owners Want from Their CPA?" *CPA Practice Advisor*, April 2014, http://www.cpapracticeadvisor.com/news/11409596/what-do-small-business-owners-want-from-their-cpa.

2. Morris Treadway, "The View from the Top," KPMG, 2015, https://home.kpmg.com/xx/en/home/insights/2015/10/view-from-top.html.

3. EY, *Finance Forte: The Future of Finance Leadership*, March 2013, www.ey.com/Publication/vwLUAssets/Finance_forte_The_Future_of_Finance_Leadership_2011/$FILE/The-Future-of-Finance-Leadership.pdf.

4. Vipal Monga, "Need an Accountant? Try a Robot Instead," *Wall Street Journal*, March 2017, http://blogs.wsj.com/cfo/2017/03/07/need-an-accountant-try-a-robot-instead/.

5. Erik Dorr, Michel Janssen, and Honorio J. Padrón III, "Understanding the Structural Changes in Employment and Talent Needs in Business Services," The Hackett Group, 2013, https://itconsultmp.net/uncategorized/understanding-the-structural-changes-in-employment-and-talent-needs-in-business-services/.

6. Monga, "Need an Accountant?"

7. James Manyika, Michael Chui, Mehdi Miremadi, Jacques Bughin, Katy George, Paul Willmott, and Martin Dewhurst, "Harnessing Automation for a Future that Works," McKinsey Global Institute, January 2017, www.mckinsey.com/global-themes/digital-disruption/harnessing-automation-for-a-future-that-works.

8. Richard Fry, "Millennials Surpass Gen Xers as the Largest Generation in U.S. Labor Force," *Fact Tank*, May 11, 2015, Pew Research Center, www.pewresearch.org/fact-tank/2015/05/11/millennials-surpass-gen-xers-as-the-largest-generation-in-u-s-labor-force/.

9. PricewaterhouseCooper (PwC), *Millennials at Work: Reshaping the Workplace*, 2011, www.pwc.com/m1/en/services/consulting/documents/millennials-at-work.pdf.

CHAPTER **2**

Bringing the Human Side to Technology

For the longest time, humans were the best accounting machines—although the process was often slow and time consuming.

While our ability to speed up the process of accounting has improved with technology, we still are dependent on the human factor. Over time, accounting became about imputing data manually, keeping up with new tax codes and the ever-increasing number of deadlines.

Technology has transformed how often we can interact with numbers. New software programs can create cleaner data management. Also, they can add other components to better track different categories of information—no matter the size of the business—as well as introduce features like multicurrency for businesses with an overseas customer base.

Nowadays, you don't have to write a custom report in a software program or in a spreadsheet for each client. Instead, you can create templates one time that can be shared across the entire practice and apply those templates to each client when appropriate. What used to take hours to create can now be generated in 15 to 20 minutes and may only require a few tweaks. Technology can even streamline how you organize your daily workday. And you can do it all from your smartphone, tablet, or even a watch.

Current technology enables us to create conversations with our clients. We can set messages to alert them in real time. For example: "Good morning, Amy. Overnight we received $12,000 from last month's outstanding invoices, and it's been utilized to fund payroll. It's Mike's three-year anniversary Friday. I've left messages for Jim Jones who owes us $6,500. Have a nice day!"

We no longer have to be solitary monks, toiling away for hours. Ironically, technology has created an opportunity for more human interaction and real-time communication.

The addition of cloud technology and accounting programs has streamlined how accountants can do business. Rather than thinking about how it changes your business by eliminating work you were used to doing, think about the ways it can change *how* you do business and create new opportunities.

The advancement in cloud technology not only saves you time but also provides the data to offer greater analysis of the client's financial position. What used to take weeks or months to do manually can now be consolidated by the cloud applications for you to review in minutes or hours. The more information you have, the more in-depth and specific advice you can offer. All this adds up to you becoming more valuable to your client.

THE OLD WAY OF DATA FLOWING VERSUS THE NEW WAY

For the longest time, accounting professionals and bookkeepers worked like this: Financial information was received from multiple sources (i.e., banks, suppliers, and customers); all this data was manually entered into the accounting software by bookkeepers or accounting professionals; then the information was coded properly or cleaned up from client entries. All of this work had to be completed before finally presenting financial reports to the client.

There are also problems associated with clients doing their own accounting when they do not have a financial background. For example, say your client does not know anything about accounting, but uses their own accounting software to create their financial statements. More times than not, the financial statements do not make sense, because the information is not coded correctly (e.g., a purchase of retail clothing is coded to office supplies rather than as an inventory asset). This just creates more of a mess that has to be cleaned up.

This was the old data flow method, and it had two major flaws: (1) it was time-consuming, and (2) it raised the odds of human error.

The new data flow method utilizes cloud technology, which helps data flow more efficiently from the banks and clients to a central program. This method eliminates much of the manual data entry and its potential for human error, and it helps ensure the integrity of the data. In addition, the new method saves a lot of valuable time and presents an opportunity to become more engaged with your clients.

This new method of processing with technology will finally allow us to have that available time to discuss the other questions clients have, besides their taxes. I hear things like this from many small business owners: "My accountant will not call me back. I want them to help me with a question I have on my business and they don't respond." Clients want and are willing to pay for this advice—you just have to set up your practice properly to respond real time and provide meaningful answers.

Why doesn't a client's accounting professional call back? Maybe the accountant doesn't have the time. Or maybe it's because the accountant is afraid that the client will ask questions to which he or she may not have the answers.

However, you don't *need* to know the answer right away. Clients don't expect you to have instant results—but they do want to pay you for your expertise and responsiveness.

So how do you become more of an expert in a client's business? By replacing the old way of doing things with the new way.

Most accountants don't like to make changes unless they are forced to do so by new pronouncements or regulatory changes. However, to become a cherished advisor, it is critical that you eliminate manual data entry and start automating as much as possible. Once you transform your practice into a smoother, more efficient operation via cloud technology, you will have much more time that you can devote to fostering stronger client relationships.

To begin the journey of transformation, you need to spend time documenting the processes in your practice so you can identify what work is manual, duplicated, or inefficient and could possibly be solved with emerging cloud technology.

For example, when you have the right technology in place, you will no longer spend time filling in timesheets at the end of the day, dealing with printing and sending statements to clients, or focusing on collections. You will not have to devote hours trying to manage work in process, sorting through what needs to be reviewed or entering data manually. This will all be automated, and you'll be notified when you need to complete a task.

Research has shown that cloud technology can be an advantage to companies. For example, in 2013, Rackspace surveyed 1,300 organizations in the United Kingdom and the United States, including 1,000 small and medium businesses and 300 companies with 1,000 employees or more. The survey covered the financial services, retail, manufacturing, professional services, and information technology (IT) industries. Here are some highlights of the survey's findings:

- 60 percent of respondents stated that the cloud has given them more time to focus on strategy and innovation.
- Almost 50 percent of respondents said that cloud technology enabled them to grow their businesses.
- 62 percent of respondents said that cloud technology enabled their companies to invest more money back into their business.[1]

The Rackspace survey also explored how companies were investing their savings from cloud technology. The top choices for large companies (62 percent) as well as small- and medium-size businesses (48 percent) were new products and service innovation.

Ask yourself this question: "What do I want to do with this time I've freed up by embracing cloud technology?" Like the Rackspace respondents, you can utilize the savings from cloud technology as an opportunity to invest in cherished advising and growing your business with new clients.

WHAT CEOs WANT FROM THEIR CFOs

As previously mentioned, a majority of chief executive officers (CEOs) believe chief financial officers (CFOs) are capable of much more than their title suggests.[2] However, even with this encouragement, CEOs tend to have little confidence that their CFOs are ready for the future. For example, more details from the 2015 KPMG Global CEO Survey cited in Chapter 1 found that 33 percent of the surveyed CEOs said that their CFOs were up to the task of taking on new challenges.[3] Also, 97 percent of the respondent CEOs in the survey said that the ability to attract and retain finance talent is the most important contribution in order to improve their company's financial ability. However, only 33 percent of the CEOs gave their CFOs a thumb up in terms of talent management. What are CEOs looking for in the CFOs? The same survey respondents said that experience with transformation and innovation is the second-most important attribute a CFO can possess (with global experience being first).

While this is just one survey, the information reflects a great opportunity for CFOs. If CFOs want to improve their value, they need to enhance key areas like leadership qualities and big-picture vision, and broaden their experience beyond finance.

This is where an investment in building a cherished advisor program can pay off, as it will rebuild the client–accountant relationships and strengthen all three of those areas.

Leadership Qualities

To be a cherished advisor, you cannot hide behind the numbers. To make it work, you must be the person who drives the interaction with the client. Part of being a leader is also identifying other accountants who would be good candidates to invest in and teaching them how to become advisors themselves. This approach will allow you to build teams and motivate them to work together to deliver these new services.

Big-Picture Vision

Becoming a cherished advisor creates an opportunity to look beyond your normal clientele and how you do business. It is not about just bringing in more clients, but looking down the road to identify what you want for your own practice, whether you want to achieve more quality of life or to grow your business. Also, assessing potential growing industries that your services will need now and in the future will help you stay ahead of technology as well as master the complexities of data analytics and discover how they can benefit both existing and potential new customers.

Broader Experience

A cherished advisor is someone who spends time understanding the intangible pieces of their client's business. As accountants we traditionally understand figures—debits and credits and how the numbers add up. A cherished advisor brings value by applying what they see and hear from the client to the numbers on the financials.

For example, the advisor becomes knowledgeable on the operational side of the business and understands how the entire operation functions from the warehouse inventory to selling goods and marketing. The advisor can talk with the client about how the business runs, what markets have the most potential, and where the client wants the business to go. The advisor then can examine the financial reports and see how they support the client's goals and the way the business runs in reality.

With insight into the business's operation and knowledge about the financial data, the cherished advisor can begin a meaningful conversation about the client's business and offer suggestions that might be able to help them. As a result, you will become an integral part of the client's business and build a long-term relationship that both you and the client can rely upon. The value you provide will be so essential to the client that they couldn't imagine not having you as a part of their operations and how they make decisions. This also sets in motion a blueprint to recruit other similar businesses by offering them this unique, personalized service.

CHOOSING YOUR VERTICAL INDUSTRY NICHE

When I work with accounting practices, I ask them what type of clients they target and what their client breakdown is by industry. Many times, their response is that they have all client industries and aren't sure about the segmentation—how many are not for profits, retail, or creative, for example.

Part of being a cherished advisor is to think beyond your normal scope of clients and identify new industries (and thus new potential clients) that match your personal interests, expertise, and knowledge—or what I call your vertical industry niche. Finding your vertical industry niche creates an opportunity to choose clients that will appreciate the services you have to offer as a cherished advisor.

Creating Your Vertical Industry Niche

The first step to identifying potential vertical industry specializations is to define your purpose. Consider the question, "Why am I interested in pursuing this particular niche?" Your purpose goes beyond wanting to bring in new business. Here, you define the motivation, personal goals, and standards for you and your practice. Identify which industries you may feel a connection to, or those which have a mission and goals you believe in.

Here's an example. Besides being a CPA, my hobby is yoga. I am a certified yoga instructor, so if I were to select a vertical industry niche, I might choose yoga studios or other health and wellness businesses because they match not only my personal interest, but also an aligned set of values to improve people's lives through health and wellness.

Another way to look at your purpose is how it would make you feel to have a particular business as a client. Would it feel like *work*—or would you enjoy the process of helping the client grow and achieve its goals, because you believe in the client's missions and values as a business?

After you have defined your purpose, you can begin to identify specific industries that might be good candidates for your vertical industry niche. I have found that there are five basic steps that can help you define this niche for your practice.

 ## HOW THE DIGITAL CPA SELECTED ITS VERTICAL INDUSTRY NICHE

The following interview was conducted by Amy Vetter with Jay Kimelman, CPA, founder, and CIO of The Digital CPA in Tampa, Florida.

What services does your practice offer?

Kimelman: The Digital CPA started in November 2011 after a "divorce" from a former business unrelated to accounting. At that time, I worked with what I knew—desktop accounting software—and like any other business starting out, I took any client who would pay. A few months later I took a call from a prospective client looking for a cloud-based GL [general ledger] that would connect to their billing software. This call transformed me. I found the cloud, and I have not looked back. Six years later, the Digital CPA is home based, has grown to a team of five, and is looking to be 100 percent cloud based soon. The last step in that evolution is tax software. We offer a range of services including:

- Bookkeeping
- Accounting
- Payroll
- Tax
- Virtual CFO and Consulting
- Cloud Conversion

How did you select your industry vertical?

Kimelman: I learned that sometimes there is a trial and error process in finding your vertical. For instance, as I had spent about half of my professional career in manufacturing and distribution, I figured that was where my client base would come from. I targeted this industry, but did not really gain any traction.

One day I was in a meeting and an attorney asked me a question regarding trust accounting. Early in my career, I spent a lot of time working for nursing home management companies and was the ace who was called in to clean up patient trust funds. Interest on Lawyer Trust Accountants, or IOLTA, is the same thing, but for lawyers. I met with the attorney and felt this was a good fit, so I made law firms my vertical.

However, after picking up a few more clients, I quickly discovered that it was not giving me joy. Even though the type of work was similar it wasn't the same. So I revisited what I loved doing, and it was building e-commerce websites. That market is growing, and so instead I'm an e-commerce CPA working with online sellers.

How did you know when you found the right industry?

Kimelman: For me it was when I felt very charged after a meeting with the owners and realizing they wanted to learn and apply what we were advising.

What did you discover about yourself and your approach to accounting during this process?

Kimelman: During this time, we grew from just myself to the team we are today. So not only were we learning new things every day, I was trying to delegate more of the work and the business development role. Delegation is easy to say, but it is much harder to do. It only takes five minutes to accomplish this certain task, so just do it. That is great when you are a sole operator, but when you are the leader, you must delegate that task and transfer the knowledge, and it will take you longer, and you have to have the faith your staff will do it right.

How did this shift change how you approached traditional accountant–client relationships? What specifically did it improve or expand on, and why was this important to your practice/business?

Kimelman: Clients no longer contact me directly. Instead, we are using the team approach, with one staff member as the Client Account Manager. We are doing this for a number of reasons. Most importantly is to pull me out of the day-to-day operations and to allow me to lead the team and deliver more profitable advisory services, which then comes with improved client service and communications. This gives us better client satisfaction and greater profitability.

How did you put together a software platform for your chosen industry vertical?

Kimelman: For e-commerce businesses, there are two technology stacks we use. This depends on sales channels. I learned from others what the best tools were for this vertical. For the other rest of the platform, it was a lot of trial and error. As a "tech junkie," I tried new apps that would make me more efficient, or be easier for my client. Trials and demos are my friend—I sign up for them all. A lot of the time, I would know in five minutes if the new app was not a fit, and I would end the trial right away. Sometimes it takes time to see if all of your needs are met.

The biggest takeaway on the right platform is that no platform is perfect. You will need to make compromises. What works for others might not work for you.

Step 1: Selection

This is about naming the various types of industries that naturally attract you, that you could see yourself working in, and that are aligned with your purpose. Often, this is based on your personal interests and professional experiences. For starters, ask yourself the following questions:

- What are your passions?
- What do you enjoy doing during your personal time?
- If you could work in any field other than accounting, what would it be?
- What are your hobbies?
- What have you done in the past year or so that really made you happy?
- If you have an existing practice, do you naturally have a concentration of clients in any one industry?

Begin making a list of the areas that you find appealing, and then match them to their industry. Do you enjoy eating out? That would be restaurants and entertainment. Do you enjoy travel? That might be travel or hospitality. Do you like to run, swim, or cycle? That would be health and fitness. Don't worry about prioritizing the list—just write down what comes to mind and don't be afraid to add something that may feel a bit "out there."

Step 2: Profitability

Next, narrow your list down to the top three to five industries. Begin to explore how profitable these industries are and whether they have grown in recent years—or have indicators that they show the potential to grow.

Sageworks, a finance information company, compiles industry data on privately held companies and produces an annual ranking of the most profitable industries. In 2016, they listed accounting, tax preparation, bookkeeping, and payroll services as the most profitable industries, with a net profit of 18.3 percent, followed by 14 other industries with a net profit margin of 10.5 percent or higher (see Table 2.1).[4] Where do your potential virtual niche industries fall in this list?

Table 2.1 Most Profitable Industries in 2016

Industry	Net Profit Margin
Accounting, Tax Preparation, Bookkeeping	18.3%
Legal Services	17.4%
Lessors of Real Estate	17.4%
Outpatient Care Centers	15.9%
Offices of Real Estate Agents and Brokers	14.8%
Offices of Other Health Practitioners	14.2%
Offices of Dentists	14.1%
Specialized Design Services	12.8%
Automotive Equipment Rental and Leasing	12.5%
Activities Related to Real Estate	12.3%
Warehousing and Storage	11.6%
Offices of Physicians	11.5%
Nonmetallic Mineral Mining and Quarrying	11.2%
Medical and Diagnostic Laboratories	11.1%

Data source: Sageworks

Step 3: Expertise

Next, explore your level of expertise within each industry that you identified as desirable. This is about how you gauge your current and possibly future knowledge of the segment. Do you already possess in-depth knowledge or have previous experience in the industry? Is it an area in which you could envision yourself succeeding if you devoted more time to it? What skills would you need to attain to have the expertise you need to serve those clients?

Step 4: Technology Fit

The next step is to assess which cloud technology will help this market and create greater efficiency for these potential clients. Explore the economics of putting this technology together and being able to offer it to a potential client. It's important to understand from prospects and clients what predominant operational cloud technologies they use in their industries. Then determine whether these technologies will integrate with a cloud accounting system so information doesn't have to be manually re-keyed.

For instance, if I pursued a yoga-studio niche, I might find that most studios primarily use the same cloud-based point-of-sale (POS) system for their scheduling, retail, and service sales because it caters to the health and wellness industry.

First, you should assess whether that system can be integrated with the cloud accounting system you want to use. Then, determine whether there are any possible technologies you would want the client to replace or implement in order to make the process more efficient. Last, assess whether your client would be open to making a switch in accounting systems, and what level of effort would be needed for training the client and his or her staff.

Step 5: Realign with Your Purpose

After you have gone through the process of analyzing the different industries, the final step should be to determine which industries might be the best candidates for your niche. Compare your research of each industry to your original purpose—or your "Why."

The reason for doing this is that during the previous steps, you might have discovered some issues that make the industries no longer align with your original intention. Is this still an area that you will still enjoy and fits your original intentions? Is there a financial impediment that would cause it to not create economic value for your practice? The business may fit your interests, but does it match the purpose and culture of your firm? Remember that your purpose pertains to yourself and your business, and you don't want a vertical industry niche to clash with either one. For instance, the business practices of a particular industry may not match your personal values, or you may discover the business might not always have the available funds to pay for your services.

HOW THE WOW COMPANY SELECTED ITS VERTICAL INDUSTRY NICHE

The following interview was conducted by Amy Vetter with Paul Bulpitt, cofounder of the WOW Company in Ampfield, United Kingdom.

How did you select your industry vertical?

Bulpitt: Sometimes the industry vertical chooses you. At WOW, we work with many creative, digital, and marketing agencies. We actually stumbled across this industry vertical. We seemed to be attracting more and more clients in this industry—predominantly through how we presented ourselves and how we work. It felt easy when working with these businesses, which is really important. This was a group of clients that our team loved working with and helping. Plus this seemed to be a profile of a business owner that valued highly the assistance and guidance we offered. Once we decided to focus on this industry, we spent time building relationships with industry thought leaders to learn more about the industry and what the most successful agencies were doing.

How did you know when you found the right industry?

Bulpitt: Finding this industry specialization was serendipitous in many ways—and other industries we have tried to target since haven't gone so well. What we discovered was that the vital ingredient is finding people to work with who believe what we believe. If that's missing, it doesn't work.

What did you discover about yourself and your approach to accounting during this process?

Bulpitt: The main lesson I've learned is that business owners engaged with their finances build better businesses. Our job evolved from getting the accounts through and answering queries, to empowering business owners to understand and be more engaged with their finances. Necessarily, your approach needs to evolve. For instance, we run training sessions for clients, and approach meetings with the goal of helping the client understand, to give clients meaningful information at their fingertips so they can make better decisions as a result. Everything we now do is focused on helping businesses thrive—not just on helping them be compliant and saving tax and meeting statutory filing requirements.

How did you put together a software platform for your chosen industry vertical?

Bulpitt: This process began in reverse. As a firm, we adopted Xero as our accountancy platform in 2009. We then looked at the next biggest headache for business owners in their finance function—paperwork. We started using Receipt Bank before it was publically launched, and it's been at the core of our platform ever since. Receipt Bank has saved our clients thousands of hours that they're now able to spend with their families or doing something much more worthwhile than processing bills and expenses. We use Spotlight Reporting and Futurli to provide insight, analytics, and alerts to clients. Finally, we use GoCardless to collect payments from clients.

What advice would you offer other accountants who want to follow the same path?

Bulpitt: Be bold. Keep innovating. Put yourself in your client's shoes. What would you want if you were in their position? Also, stop trying to be all things to all people. Figure out what you're good at, what you love doing, and stick to it. Don't be afraid to turn away business. Focus on the business you want.

Looking back would you have done anything differently?

Bulpitt: Two things:

> Number 1: Pace of change. At times we have taken more time than necessary to implement change. In hindsight, we have underestimated the ability of our team to assimilate change and move on. The feedback has been to make bigger moves, faster.

Number 2: People. When we started WOW, I thought technical expertise, customer experience, and processes would determine success. However, what I've learned is that it's all about our people and our culture. I would go back and be much clearer about our values and purpose and refuse to compromise.

SWOT Analysis

Once you have settled on three to five industries, conduct a SWOT analysis to dive a little deeper. SWOT stands for *strengths, weaknesses, opportunities, and threats,* and serves as a first step to any kind of company action—for example, exploring new initiatives, identifying areas for change, or redirecting efforts in the middle of a plan.[5] An analysis can answer key questions in identifying a vertical market, such as the following:

- Is there room for growth in that particular industry or market?
- Is the market too small to succeed—or too large to even really matter?
- What are the competitive landscape and economics of the potential clientele to want and be able to afford these services?

To begin a SWOT analysis, create a table with four columns that lists each impacting element and then compare the results.[6] For example, Table 2.2 shows what a SWOT analysis might look like if I were deciding to enter into the health and wellness vertical industry for my practice.

After you conduct the SWOT analysis, study the results and decide whether these are markets you still want to pursue. Is there enough to work with, or is there too much competition? Would you be successful targeting a client in that industry?

After you have completed this process for three to five markets, choose one—and only one—industry to start with. If you try too many industries at once, you will be taking on too much and setting yourself up for failure. This way, you can test one vertical industry niche and learn the process of developing it. Once you have that down, going into a second and third one later will be so much easier because you

Table 2.2 Health and Wellness SWOT Analysis

Strengths	Weaknesses	Opportunities	Threats
Expertise in the health and wellness industry	Many of these businesses struggle to be profitable	Participation within a growing market	Lack of immunity to an economic downturn
Existing clients in that industry to use for benchmarking	Need high volume of prospecting and sales processes, so there are always new clients to replace those that go out of business	Client opportunities all over the country and internationally, if proper cloud technology is deployed	Potential competition from larger, well-established corporations and franchises that may acquire small businesses
Aligns with personal values—helping health and wellness clients succeed sustains their businesses, so they can help more of their customers live healthier lives	Business practices need to be closely watched	Can differentiate from many other accounting practices by demonstrating the focus and expertise in this industry, which creates a higher value service	A probability that clients may go out of business
Staff has an interest and desire to learn more about the vertical industry	Business owners do not have as much financial acumen and will need a lot of training and support		
The health and wellness market is a booming industry and new businesses are being opened every day			
Business owners need the advisory services, as the financial side is not their expertise			

already have an existing framework. Even if your chosen industry does not work out, you will have created a model that you can then follow for another potential niche.

STEPS TO CREATE YOUR CLOUD PLATFORM

The final phase for creating your virtual industry niche is creating your cloud platform. This is the general ledger software accounting system you will use, along with any other add-on cloud programs that you or your client may require. The technology you choose will enable you to deliver new advisory services and provide information to your client on a real-time basis.

There are four main measurements to assess for ultimate success when choosing the technology:

Real-Time Data

Each party has their own access into the same data and files. This ensures that your client can get the most up-to-date information about their business on a daily basis. By sharing the data through the cloud with the client, this creates an advisory situation where accounting professionals can provide valuable advice to the business owner when they need it.

Efficiency

Reduce data-entry time and errors by connecting the data sources via the selected cloud technology. Data flows in for you and your clients to approve, rather than requiring manual entry. See Figure 2.1 for an example of how your connected platform may look.

Revenue

Offer higher-value services by having financial and operational visibility over more of the business. For example, accessing the cloud point-of-sale software gives you the ability to drill into specific transactions or groups of transactions, rather than looking at just an ending balance.

Growth

Combine your cloud technology with add-ons to create vertical solutions and offer vertical-specific services. These better position your practice to appeal to specific groups of potential clients by showing them the type of information they will have at their fingertips when they work with you.

Your platform is important because it focuses on several underlying areas, needs, and goals that are essential for the cloud technology's

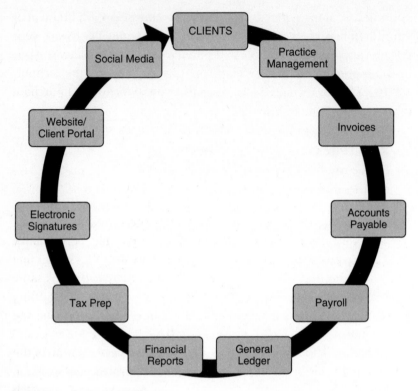

Figure 2.1 Connected Platform

success for both you and your client. For example, it addresses the following:

- Automate tasks
- Create staff efficiency
- Expand your geographic reach
- Tap into virtual resources within your practice or firm
- Work more efficiently from anywhere, anytime
- Integrate with any number of other applications (customer relationship management [CRM], payroll, billing, etc.)
- Develop effective repeatable internal processes and procedures
- Provide a consistent client experience
- Foster a collaborative workflow
- Operate to scale

When working with cloud software vendors, it's important that you do your homework first. Rather than allowing a software vendor to lead you through a sales process, come to the table with your research prepared and clear requests of what you need the technology to do for you. That will better enable you to make good purchase decisions.

To ensure cloud platform success, there are six specific steps that you should follow when evaluating software.

Step 1: Review the Status Quo

Document everything that the client does that creates data (e.g., payroll, social media, e-mail calendar, accounts payable, performance reports, tax preparation, etc.), and map out how data flows from one system to another or whether it is manually entered. Do this same process for your practice, as well, to ensure you are not duplicating work internally and to find ways to save time when preparing the financial data.

As part of reviewing the status quo, you also need to address the policies and procedures required for your platform to be successful. From a platform perspective, there are many moving parts, and each part requires a documented procedure so you can understand its value across the entire platform—as well as detail its most efficient use. The number of potential processes in your platform depends on the services you offer and what clients you want to attract. It is essential that these processes be connected and/or automated so both you and your client can access the same data. This will increase efficiency and strengthen communication between you and the client.

Step 2: Identify Pain Points and Opportunities

Determine the areas that are your client's weakest or that need the most improvement. For instance, he or she might struggle with paperwork, tracking invoices, or offering alerts. You often can find the areas that require the greatest attention by simply speaking with your client and even talking with their vendors. Also identify the top challenges you want the software to solve. This way, when you reach out to cloud software vendors, you know what you need and can determine whether the software programs they offer will meet your needs. Rank all of your requirements so that when you meet with a vendor for the first time, you can let them know your top three priorities. That way, if they can't provide a solution to those, you can move on to a different software vendor and not spend too much time reviewing features that aren't as important for your practice and/or clients.

Step 3: Identify Areas Where Technology Can Do the Heavy Lifting

Highlight the areas that could be automated or connected to your cloud system. Is there additional cloud technology that could make these areas more efficient? If technology already exists for those areas, does it need to be upgraded or switched out?

Step 4: Conduct Due Diligence of Products and Vendors

Talk to other people in the industry who have used systems you are interested in. Read reviews, meet vendors, and attend conferences to educate yourself as much as possible.

Step 5: Conduct a Test or Pilot Program

Request a demo file or trial copy so you can test the software with your own data before making a decision, rather than just relying on a sales demo.

Step 6: Review the Program's Success and Return on Investment

Did the program meet your original criteria for success? If not, determine what part of the program needs to be fixed or whether you need to replace it with another program. Keep this process agile—even if you find a fit, you may identify a technology one or two years later that can create an even better outcome. When everything is documented, it is easier to replace technology when you need to as your practice grows.

You also need to assess whether there is a return on investment (ROI) on the purchase of the software. Calculate what your total cost of ownership (TCO) is today for the software and manual processing that you do. TCO includes things such as cost of software, servers, backups, software-maintenance costs, upgrades, the time it takes to process transactions, etc. When assessing a new technology, you can calculate the new TCO and then determine the ROI by replacing what you do today with the new cloud technology and process. It may be time savings, acquisition of new clients, less TCO, or something similar. Performing this type of assessment will help you make an informed decision when selecting new technology.

THE CHERISHED ADVISOR JOURNEY

The journey of a cherished advisor seldom follows a straight path from a traditional accountant to that of a cherished advisor. There are many stages along the way. Each one is essential because it exposes you to various skills and practical experience you need to move to the next stage. As you begin integrating cloud technology and finding your vertical industry niche, it is a good idea to track your journey in terms of where your practice stands with its transformation progress.

Here is a breakdown of five typical phases accounting practices go through with this journey. This will help you gauge where you stand today and what next steps are ahead of you to get to the next milestone.

Traditional Practice

- Desktop software or server based
- Compliance based
- Static or declining client base
- Time-based billing
- No website or social media presence
- Paper-filing system
- Hard to hire new staff

Online Testing

- Dabbling in cloud
- Desktop software and server based, possibly hosted

- Some marketing
- Basic website and no social media
- Compliance-centric services
- Time-based billing
- Client base is static
- Some scanning of documents
- Research and testing of cloud general ledger applications

Cloud Entrant

- New clients on cloud applications
- Well-built website and social presence
- Investment in marketing
- Offering of advisory services
- Bundling of compliance services with other offerings
- Expansion of client base beginning
- Internal cloud champion
- Working toward full paperless

Practice Automation

- Shifting of existing clients to cloud
- Practice applications almost all in the cloud
- Interactive website
- Strategy for social media
- Fixed fees, value pricing model, advisory revenue
- Active client base, in terms of referrals
- Mostly paperless
- Introduction of add-ons to integrate with cloud accounting

Cherished Advisor

- Innovative marketing
- Proactive, real-time advice for clients
- Value billing
- Virtual CFO approach

- Less reliance on compliance service revenue
- Majority of clients in the cloud
- 100 percent cloud based and paperless
- Attracting talent from all generations

HOW WK COMPANY EMBRACED ITS NEW ROLE AS ADVISOR

The following interview was conducted by Amy Vetter with Neil Sinclair, Director of WK Advisors & Accountants in Blenheim, New Zealand.

How did you approach your new role as an advisor? Was there any trial-and-error aspect?

Sinclair: The mind-set of a business advisor needs to be different. Accountants typically think they need to come up with all the answers. A great business advisor coaches clients to come up with the answers themselves. We have now really drummed into our team, "Coaching, Not Consulting." We also found we had to go back to step one and redefine our culture. Staff had to be aware and 100 percent comfortable with our key values. Our team actually came up with our core value during a workshop. To me, this was the single biggest breakthrough that we made. Our values are:

- Accessible
- Dedication
- Vibrant
- Integrity
- Caring
- Excellence

You will see the first letter of each value forms the word *ADVICE*. So even in our core values, advisory is at the center of everything we do.

We also realized that a lot of our team would not have the skills and confidence to offer full advisory services. So we redefined our advisory services and split into two sections: financial advisory and strategic advisory. This was to recognize that providing management reporting and interpretation of key financial information was indeed also advisory.

We also discovered that we had to better educate our clients. It was a big shock for many clients that had dealt with us for years that we now operated differently. Often, the clients were not simply prepared for those conversations. I found clients often called three months later wanting another appointment, as they liked what we discussed, but did not get full value from it.

What about your approach to serving as an advisor did your clients best respond to?

Sinclair: Our more sophisticated clients loved the 90-day action plan approach where we helped them identify three to four goals they need to achieve in their business in the next 90 days. They also loved the fact that we were meeting with them regularly and assisting them to work on all aspects of their business. I also believe clients do truly appreciate the bespoke approach that we take. If you are going to do advisory properly, you owe it to your clients to upskill in key business advisory techniques and be able to assist the client to address any issues they are having. Don't just go off a script. You always need to remember, you are there to coach and not consult.

What did you discover about yourself and your approach to accounting during this process? What did you specifically learn that changed how you approached new clients, how you did business, and the like?

Sinclair: To help with our advisory skills, we utilize Mindshop, an Australian-based organization that provides advisory tools, training, and platforms to business advisory. They have a tool called the Bike of Life. This challenges you to look at the balance in your life and what you do in your business, too. We discovered that we were not working on our business enough, particularly around staff development, marketing, and strategy. So we have changed that.

The back wheel of the bike is your personal life. I found I was way out of balance. For example, while I spend quality time with the family, I did not put enough emphasis on self-development and health. So since doing the Bike of Life on myself, I have lost 55 pounds through my fitness regime, and at the same time, invested 300 hours into my self-development. Having the right tools and training, I find I am now much more confident when meeting clients and can see the value that I add, when historically, this value would not have been identified, or charged for.

What advice would you offer other accountants who want to follow the advisory path?

Sinclair: Just do it! Lots of accountants say they are business advisors, but they are not doing it consistently. You need to find a way to build your style of advisory into your core services. Don't have an advisory team, because in my view, it does not work. But before you decide to move into business advisory, define what advisory actually means to you.

And then make sure you have your core values right. We made more progress after working hard on our core values and coming up with our ADVICE values. Also, I would strongly recommend finding other firms on the same journey and working together. We have enjoyed a tight relationship with a couple of key organizations and firms, and that has helped us drive forward.

Looking back, would you have done anything differently?

Sinclair: I would certainly spend more time understanding the advisory continuum. We initially tried to move everyone to strategic advisory. We did not appreciate or value the advisory offerings in the layers from clarity to accountability. That failed. I also think we would recognize our team's strengths and limitations more, and not devalue the really important steps in the pyramid between compliance and innovation. The other key learning would be preparing clients for the change. We did nothing, so the impact was not as good as it could have been. We now have come up with some great strategies to address this.

SUMMARY

The human side of accounting will never go away, no matter how advanced technology becomes. In fact, we need human skills more than ever in accounting. By changing how they process, organize, and manage data through cloud technology, accountants can save valuable time that used to be spent on more manual tasks. This extra time can be used as an opportunity to pursue new business ventures, like a cherished advisory project. CFOs are primed to pursue this kind of endeavor as they have both the necessary skills and the encouragement and challenge of CEOs to pursue new initiatives. Identifying these new vertical markets for cherished advisors can begin by focusing on your individual interests. From there, you can conduct a more in-depth analysis, such as a SWOT analysis, and then work toward outlining a strategy on how to create an individual software program designed to fit your vertical market's specific needs.

ENDNOTES

1. Louis Columbus, "Making Cloud Computing Pay," Forbes.com, April 2013, www
.forbes.com/sites/louiscolumbus/2013/04/10/making-cloud-computing-pay-2/#
69a28a8a5656.

2. EY, *2011 Finance Forte: The Future of Finance Leadership*, 2013, www.ey.com/Publication/vwLUAssets/Finance_forte_The_Future_of_Finance_Leadership_2011/$FILE/The-Future-of-Finance-Leadership.pdf.

3. KPMG, "New Study by KPMG International Reveals Nearly One-Third of Global CEOs Feel Their CFOs Are Not Up to the Challenge," November 2015, https://home.kpmg.com/xx/en/home/media/press-releases/2015/11/kpmg-study-cfos-not-up-to-the-challenge.html.

4. Entrepreneur Staff, "The 15 Most Profitable Small-Business Industries," Sageworks, August 28, 2016, www.sageworks.com/pressroom.aspx?article=2012&title=The-15-most-profitable-small-business-industries&date=August-28-2016.

5. Nicole Fallon, "SWOT Analysis: What It Is and When to Use It," *Business News Daily*, March 28, 2017, http://www.businessnewsdaily.com/4245-swot-analysis.html.

6. Palo Alto Software, "Health Fitness Marketing Plan," 1996–2017, www.mplans.com/health_fitness_marketing_plan/situation_analysis_fc.php.

CHAPTER 3

The Cherished Advisor

The Transformation Journey beyond the Technology

To *cherish* means to hold dear, to be treasured or valued. As accounting professionals, we go into this profession to help our clients thrive, and the ultimate goal is that they feel we have provided them with the value they paid for. The foundation for becoming a cherished advisor is how you develop and manage your relationship with your client. This interaction between accountants and clients goes beyond cloud technology, data, and figures. It is about delivering value that a client needs from you as an accounting professional, such that the client can't imagine not having you as part of the business. You are that crucial to their success.

Many accountants offer the same type of tax and financial reports that you can, but what makes you a cherished advisor is that you become an integral part of the client's operations. Your client seeks you out for advice and counsel to help make the real business decisions that he or she needs help with during the month. He or she is invested in your insight because you offer advice about their business through a different lens.

Another way to think about being a cherished advisor is moving away from tangible services to intangible ones. A tangible service is something your client can see, like a financial report or tax report. The intangible is the learning you do about your client's business—not only knowing the financial side, but also understanding the client's operations—this creates differentiation in your services.

Many kinds of skills are needed to provide services beyond the financial statements. The skills often are dictated by the client's industry, but many apply across the board. Some of the required skills are communication, analysis, leadership, problem-solving, collaboration, and teamwork. You can often develop these through personal improvement, continuous education, and hands-on learning.

For example, in your role as a cherished advisor, you become more engrossed in the client's business operations. For instance, you may gain a clear understanding of the client's inventory, and from that you may be able to pinpoint problems of oversupply that the client wouldn't have recognized as the reason for the high inventory value on their balance sheet. By pointing out the inventory issue and offering a solution, you can help the client overcome a financial obstacle. The client does not necessarily see the time and effort you put into learning about their inventory operations, but he or she will see the end results by getting a more complete analysis of their financial statements on which they can take action.

DOCUMENTING THE BUSINESS PROCESSES

As discussed in Chapter 2, "Bringing the Human Side to Technology," there is a process you should follow to help identify the right accounting platform for your chosen vertical industry niche. However, before you take the steps to implement your chosen platform, you need to document the client's business processes. This documentation will provide a map you can follow to learn where the gaps are and what needs the most attention when implementing new technology.

Documenting the processes and business practices also creates a template that you can use as a benchmark for all possible future clients in that vertical industry. In the beginning of a client relationship, it is important to conduct on-site or remote meetings and observations in order to witness how each department is involved with the daily business operations and how they affect financial outcomes.

Conducting a Client Interview

Formalizing the client interview process in the beginning of an engagement is important to ensure that the needs of the client are documented and that important information isn't lost. During the interview, ask the client to walk you through his/her day-to-day business practices. What is done and in what order? Make sure that the client does not skip a step or think a task is insignificant. Here are some guidelines to follow to ensure you are properly prepared:

Pre-interview Strategies:
- Interview the client to assess his or her skill level and the condition of their accounting records.

- Document everything so that you can revisit the interview periodically during your business dealings with the client.

- Make sure your initial meetings with a prospective client are bidirectional, where both you and the client ask questions. Ensure you are doing more questioning than just providing answers.

- Always be mindful that the client is evaluating you as well—your reputation, your experience, your personnel, and your skills.

Basic Information to Cover in Your Interview:

- Contact and company information
- Previous accountant and/or consultant relationships
- Income tax return history
- Accounting goals
- Licenses, users, and networks
- Payroll preparation history
- Sales and customer information
- Sales tax information
- Inventory
- Computer hardware and software utilized
- Insight into the client's current data file setup

For the actual interview, it is a good idea to follow a template with your questions and the client's answers documented. That way, any person who is conducting the interview asks the same questions, so your firm will acquire the same basis of information you need for any client. This list acts as a checklist to ensure you ask about all the information you need, and it keeps the responses organized so you can easily return to them when needed. The checklist should also include the following information:

- Contact information
- Technology infrastructure
- Current chart of accounts

- Future accounting file needs
- Third-party solution selection
- Inventory specifications
- Users and permission setup
- Customer list
- Vendors/contractors list
- Employee list
- Opening balances
- Accounting reports needed
- Estimates and sales orders
- Purchase orders
- Invoicing and receiving payments setup
- Merchant services
- Forms/letters to customize
- Bank reconciliations needed
- Fixed assets list
- Accounts payable (A/P) setup
- Sales tax setup
- Loans payable/lines of credit outstanding
- Due to/from accounts and balances
- Payroll setup or solution utilized
- Memorized transactions listing
- Planning and budgeting process
- Financial statements setup
- Closing of accounting periods process
- Setup and training

The specific information you gather for each section depends on the client and the industry. Again, the goal is to have as much information as possible about the client's financial infrastructure. Table 3.1 shows an example of the kind of questions you would ask a client regarding their payroll setup to get a full understanding of the process.

Table 3.1 Payroll Client Interview Checklist

Outside payroll company:					
Name of the person that processes payroll:					
What is the frequency of your payroll? (Circle one.)	Weekly	Biweekly	Semimonthly	Monthly	Other
Do you prepare your own W-2s?	Yes	No			
Do you track employees by department?	Yes	No			
Do you track employees by workers comp classification?	Yes	No			
Do you job-cost your payroll expenses?	Yes	No			
Do you produce certified payroll?	Yes	No			
Do you offer direct deposit?	Yes	No			
Are employees working in different states?	Yes	No			
Do you offer benefits?	Yes	No			
Do you have union employees?	Yes	No			
Do you have local taxes?	Yes	No			
Do you track sick, vacation, and/or personal time?	Yes	No			
Do you need to track overtime?	Yes	No			
How is time recorded in the field?					
How do you track commissions?					

Following Up after the Interview

After you have conducted your client interview, document your findings. For instance:

- Create a good list from your conversations of what each of the departments do. This includes everything from sales to A/P to procurement to customer service.
- Break down the steps of how information flows within each department. For example, for the sales department, document the routine used for contacting potential customers, sending out proposals, and writing contracts.

Next, you should shadow the business. Spend time observing each department in action. Schedule meetings with each department and ask each person to do his or her normal everyday tasks while you watch and observe. Many times, what is said during an interview is how everyone thinks business processes are occurring. However, once you see the employees in action, you pick up where certain tasks are not done in the way they were intended or where duplication of work is happening.

Also, talking with employees from each department, and watching them perform their tasks, can help you get better insight. Here are some questions you may want to ask:

- Can you explain your daily job in detail from beginning to end?
- Why do you do transactions a certain way?
- What do you think is the most time-consuming activity and why?
- What are the biggest problems or frustrations in your job?
- What works best and why?
- What would you change to improve your job and why?

HOW UPSOURCED ACCOUNTING MOVED TO ADVISORY SERVICES

The following interview was conducted by Amy Vetter with Ryan Watson, CPA, Founder and Principal of Upsourced Accounting in Columbus, Ohio.

How did you identify the skill sets you needed to change from compliance-oriented work to advisory services?

Watson: In the early days, winning new clients was difficult. We were approaching the market, and our first engagements, with our Big 4 compliance hats on—implementing controls, complex processes, and unnecessary accruals for businesses that not only didn't need them, but didn't have time to bother with them. After a few months of beating our heads against the wall—both because our message wasn't resonating with prospects and because our current clients just didn't seem to love what it was we were doing—we lifted our heads and asked, "What are we doing wrong?" And I think the big epiphany for us is we realized we were approaching the market with a one-size-fits-all view of what they needed to do without instead trying to understand their goals and what they were trying to accomplish. Advisory services, in a way, are like business therapy. You have to have empathy for and understand the business owner's problem before you can even begin proposing solutions. The minute we did more listening and less talking was the turning point for us to really begin embracing a true advisory approach.

Walk through the process of when you first established a relationship with your client that was not just compliance, but where you began to learn the operational side of what the client does. What was that like, what were the steps you went through to understand the business, and what did you discover?

Watson: This first relationship was with our first client—a fast casual salad restaurant. After several months of service, we decided to restart, and we paid a visit to the restaurant.

After a few minutes of conversation it was clear where their concerns were. The owners were two young guys with limited restaurant experience and no good sense or muscle memory around to know which results were "good" and which were "bad." And with the razor-thin margins of restaurants, there was little room for error.

So we dug in. First was to benchmark them against a few publicly traded restaurants in their category, such as Pei Wei and Chipotle. Neither were perfect comparisons, but they were enough to identify a glaring issue—food costs. Our client was spending 30 percent to 40 percent more on food than recommended.

Now that we'd identified that margin was the issue, we took to both top line and COGS [cost of goods sold] to understand the breakpoints for each. A quick analysis of menu prices against the market in their area gave us a good sense they were pushing the top end of market demand, and there would be no way to fix food margin by raising prices. The only option was to reduce costs.

The problem was we weren't sure where to reduce. Was it portions? Was it specific ingredients?

With the help of the owner, we broke down food costs by ingredient and by item to gain a better understanding. We knew costs were too high on average, but were they too high categorically, or were there specific culprits responsible for the issue? Turns out only a small handful of the choices were driving the majority of the cost overrun, and the commonality among these menu items? Goat cheese. They were using a locally sourced goat cheese that when added to a menu item made it financially unsustainable. Coming out of that analysis, we took two actions:

We added a small upcharge for goat cheese, and we implemented a half salad at half the size, but for two-thirds to three-quarters the price of a full salad, which resulted in a higher margin.

The result? Within a few short months, the food costs fell within a reasonable range. The half salads were a hit, and we found customers loved the goat cheese addition so much they were willing to pay extra for it.

We learned a surprisingly simple lesson with that first client we've taken to heart with each client thereafter—listen first, speak second.

Once you discovered the skills you needed, how did you determine where to go for further education? What helped you to make this decision and why?

Watson: For us, it was all real-world. We were good at the technical work behind the advisory services—we had built plenty of models; we understood cash flow, budgeting, and forecasting; and we were well equipped to perform the tax planning. What differentiates great advisory from mediocre advisory is client service. It is knowing what questions to ask, listening carefully to the responses, and problem-solving for unique situations on the fly. It's clearly communicating next steps, setting the right expectations, and developing the systems and repeatable processes to deliver the solution. All of these things can be perfected through repetition.

Our goal was to put our company in as many positions to practice as possible. We were intentional about leaving our comfort zone and talking with other businesses. We volunteered to teach classes for entrepreneurial support organizations and startup accelerators. We hosted small business lunches where we invited several businesses to our office each week to chat about a topic, hear their struggles, and brainstorm practical ways to mitigate or solve.

Naturally each of these activities served the dual purpose of filling our marketing funnel, but they were also important practice for our team to ask questions, listen, empathize, and creatively problem solve.

Once you further developed these skills, how did you apply them to your client's operations? Is there a formalized process that you now go through with each client to learn more about their operations so you can better advise them?

Watson: Once we felt like we understood this model, we invested a lot of time perfecting the onboarding process. Onboarding is the opportunity to slow down, understand the client needs, and develop the strategy and the systems to deliver the advisory. If you rush through onboarding, the engagement is often not set up for success, and once that happens, there is no coming back.

Our onboarding consists of a few steps:

1. **Proposal:** The first is a proposal document, complete with a video, team bios, and process documents that clearly set expectations for how we work and what we do. Proper expectation setting is one of the keys to a successful advisory engagement, and we hit this right out of the gate.
2. **New client survey:** We take new clients through a comprehensive survey to collect basic information about their business, the key contacts, and the services

we'll be performing. The intent here is to strip the "administrative" stuff away so that when we do meet, we can focus on the meat and the narrative and not get mired in the weeds of phone numbers and EINs [Employer Identification Numbers].

3. **Kick-off call:** Once we have a completed survey and engagement letter, we host a kickoff call that we leverage to understand our client's classes of transactions and processes. This is where we ask questions not just about how things are done, but more importantly, what information or risks are truly important to the business owner at every step.

4. **Implementation:** After the kickoff call, we take the information from the business and develop processes and select applications. We document the flow of information, and we develop our own internal checklists to be able to deliver on the process. We'll meet once more with the business owner to discuss our selections and train the team on the applications, as necessary. We also take this opportunity to walk through a build of a financial model. The model is the core of our service offering. Every period end result is compared to the model; any changes in the business are reflected in the model; and our collective success or failure is measured against the model. This is our roadmap.

How do you price and package these services?

Watson: Our packages and pricing are done client by client after one or more exploratory conversations. There was a time we maintained specific packages with standard, published pricing and predefined service offerings, but we've migrated away from that. I believe a lot of the learning for us about what makes an effective advisory service is the appreciation that one size doesn't fit all. Some of our clients need us to be their CFO, and others need us to augment an existing one. Some clients are extremely cash sensitive, and need weekly cash flow planning conversations, and others have several months of operating capital in the bank and don't need to manage cash flow as closely. Every client is different. Even the manner in which we deliver bill payment varies substantially client to client.

Looking back, what would you have done differently in terms of developing these skills and why?

Watson: We would have prioritized these advisory skills from the beginning. In the first year or two of our firm, we severely underpriced our work. By underpricing what we did, we applied pressure on ourselves to earn a margin at low rates, and therefore limited the amount of time we felt like we could spend onboarding and servicing a client. When your pricing forces you to deliver generalized, commodity work, you leave yourself little opportunity to develop (or deliver) these skills. As a result, we really shortchanged our own development. It wasn't until we began charging for proper advisory services that we gave ourselves the freedom and flexibility to develop the skillset.

OBTAINING NEEDED TECHNICAL AND BUSINESS SKILLS

Once you document the client's entire business process, then you can move onto the next stage: identifying the extra technical and business skills you need to best serve your client. A cherished advisor requires skills that go beyond basic accounting principles and software platforms. Your intangible services include in-depth knowledge in the business operations. For example:

Technical Skills:
- Cost accounting
- Business planning
- Cash flow management
- Budgeting
- Financial statement analysis versus traditional tax compliance
- Write-up and payroll

Business Skills:
- Process improvement
- Project management
- Forecasting
- Analysis communication
- Sales and marketing

The learning begins here in order to shift how you deliver services. It is sometimes hard to move beyond the mind-set of staying with what you know to making the decision to become a beginner again and attain the technical and business skills needed to become a cherished advisor.

By documenting the business process, you can also better identify the areas where you need improvement or further education (either because you are a novice or have some experience but need more). There are several ways to do this, including the following:

Take Additional Classes Through an Association or Community College

You can also attend classes at either a university (online or in-person) or at day or weeklong continuing education programs. There are many courses offered in adult learning programs at college institutions on the technical and business skills listed above. Set a goal of taking at least one course a quarter or in a weekend or night program to help develop these skills. Additionally, most national accounting organizations like the American Institute of Certified Public Accountants (AICPA, at aicpa.org) and the Certified Global Management Accountant (CGMA, at cgma.org) also offer training programs and certification programs you can take advantage of to learn these skills.

Reach Out to the Business Community

Devote time to visit other small businesses owners in your community and interview them about their stores, their goals, their challenges, and their successes. This can help you polish your interaction skills with potential clients as well as practice methods to receive information and offer insight.

Enlist a Mentor

Find an individual in your industry with the expertise you need. You can also join industry-related social media groups on LinkedIn and Facebook and ask questions on these forums. You can select people whom you respect for their knowledge and offer to pay them as a "coach" on your first engagements so you have someone to ask questions. This investment would be similar to paying for classes or courses, but it provides you access to someone who has the experience you are looking for and who will be available to you when you need him or her.

Use Your Audit Experience

Many of us start out in audit or tax in our accounting careers. I have found that my audit experience has been invaluable in helping me to be a good advisor. The skills you learn as an auditor can be put to good use in this service line. Knowing how to investigate discrepancies, question staff on their business processes, and understand internal controls and operational activities such as inventory management will provide the knowledge that will assist you in an advisory role.

Get Certified

Many software vendors have developed their own educational programs to help you become proficient on their software. These curriculums are often included in the partner programs you sign up for. Take advantage of these valuable resources and spend the right amount of time learning the software and understanding what that software solves for your clients or yourself. This is a time investment that is necessary and pays off in the future. It's harder to try to figure it out on your own, plus it will take you more time, instead of allowing yourself to be walked through step by step. Plus, you can advertise your certifications as additional qualifications to potential clients.

Get Hands-on Experience

Reach out to other industry colleagues or businesses in the same field as your vertical industry niche and ask to do work for them. When I started my practice, I looked for other advisors in my area and offered my services on a per diem basis. This allowed me to learn what the engagements were like, what questions clients ask and how to do the work. You can ask to shadow on specific engagements you want to learn, such as budgeting, cash-flow planning, client engagement, or sales presentations. In exchange, you can offer your accounting services either as a direct trade or at a discounted rate, since this is a learning opportunity for you.

You will soon find that every client has different needs or wants to have different levels of involvement. Hands-on learning will help you to identify any knowledge gaps you may have, so that you can fill them either by gaining experience doing the work or by taking classes that apply to your needs.

 ## HOW GUNNCHAMBERLAIN MOVED TO ADVISORY SERVICES

The following interview was conducted by Amy Vetter with Shelly Lingor, CPA, Director of Technology Solutions at GunnChamberlain in Ponte Vedra, Florida.

How did you identify the skill sets you needed to change from compliance-oriented work to advisory services?

Lingor: Forward thinking and technology are the keys to shifting from compliance to advisory services. The programs and systems that companies use have to be state-of-the-art and have to be consistently updated to deliver the best products and options for our clients. We also must have staff and people that can think outside of the traditional workflow process and bring technology and automation into the process.

Can you walk us through the process of when you first established a relationship with your client that was not just compliance, but where you began to learn the operational side of what the client does? What was that like, what were the steps you went through to understand the client's business, and what did you discover?

Lingor: First, find their pain point—what keeps them up at night? Is it the economics—anything from cash flow to overhead—or not knowing how the company is performing, and they want more insight into what is going on? Business owners usually have the "feel" that something is right or working, but they don't know how to solve issues or problems. Getting to know your clients—being honest and having them agree to invest in making the processes/systems better—is key to making a relationship work for both sides.

Once you know the pain point, you can introduce the process that will make their company better and be able to deliver a "value add" service that benefits both parties and make the relationship work for years to come. In today's world, I feel the solution is relationships and technology.

For example, I had a client with multiple locations, and each location would have to enter expenses into an older system and send the payable invoices via e-mail or standard mail (yes, some people still use that!) to get approval; then they could process for payment.

We put systems and apps in place in which everyone could see real-time data and do approvals for payables on the same day, and it cut the payable process down by two weeks. Not only did it help the payable process, it allowed the company to have updated financials and let them actually plan their cash flow instead of looking at the business 30 to 60 days later. The client saw the value and benefits of outsourcing the accounting, so that we could give our client the necessary information to make good business decisions.

Once you discovered the skills you needed, how did you determine where to go for further education (this can be academic, real world, or combo)? What helped you to make this decision and why?

Lingor: You have to invest in staff being able to master the different technology programs/software and becoming "masters" with them. Investing in staff is the most important. Technology/software is always evolving and changing, so you have to look at alternative ways to keep your staff up to date with their certifications and with new programs coming out. I think that technology/accounting conferences are a great way to educate your team and also expose them to new programs/systems, enabling your firm to stay at the forefront of technology and the solutions. Personal experience at the conferences really showed me the value of attending and the education that is associated with them.

Can you discuss what the education process was like and what you learned?

Lingor: Education was easy for me because I identified and found the programs/software packages that I really believed in and invested my time in them to learn and master. I love the hands-on/small-group sessions that really let you identify and talk about what challenges you have had. Also, others might have had the same experience and they share that; you can learn so much from colleagues and what they have been through.

Once you further developed these skills, how did you apply them to your client's operations? Is there a formalized process that you now go through with each client to learn more about their operations so you can better advise them?

Lingor: First you have to identify the correct clients that can use the solution. Some clients are set in their ways and are not always the best for newer solutions. You have to accept that and try not to push it on those clients because it will not work. You will both become frustrated and it will not work. You have to find the right clients for the right solutions. Once you can do that, then it is easy to present, train, and adapt your clients to new ways and technology. Otherwise, you will fail and go back to your old ways, and not become the financial advisor that you want to be. Once you have the right clients, you will realize that the "old" clients who are not willing to adapt take too much of your time and are not worth it. Knowing your clients, knowing what they need, and knowing how you can help is the most valuable service you can offer them. If they are not willing to listen—are they really a good client?

How do you price and package these services?

Lingor: Value pricing is the only way to do it. What value are you giving your clients, and what is it worth to them? What is it worth to you? You can take a traditional "after the fact" accounting client—do their bank recs (60 days later or even at year end), tie out their balance sheet, and do their tax return—but at the end of the day, what value did you give the client? Yes, you did their tax return, but if you had a real time status of the business, just imagine what advice and direction you could give throughout the year to make the business more profitable. I feel this is a valuable service that doesn't come with just compliance or accounting services; it comes when you offer advisory services for your client and can help your client make better business decisions.

Looking back, what would you have done differently in terms of developing these skills, and why?

Lingor: I would have gone with a firm that was more forward thinking and would have allowed the technology to come into place four years ago when it took off—and not go "back" to traditional accounting/compliance. This way we could really become a partner with clients and value that relationship and advise them to embrace technology and create the efficiencies that can be made when you connect with the right accounting solution provider.

NEW STAFFING MODEL

The next step in your learning process is to structure how you create job descriptions and organize the staff in your practice. It's an opportunity to create a new way for people to work together as teams, collaborate, and learn from each other.

The rapidly changing workforce has created an ideal opportunity to make these changes internally. Today, approximately 70 percent of the workforce are millennials—those born between 1983 and 1999.

This group offers many of the key characteristics your team needs to succeed. For instance, millennials are more engaged in emerging technology than any group of workers. A report from PricewaterhouseCoopers (PwC) entitled "Millennials at Work: Reshaping the Workplace" found that 59 percent of millennials often look at a potential employer's provision of technology when considering employment, and 78 percent said using technology they like makes them more effective.[1]

Millennials are also looking for opportunities to grow. They are not necessarily motivated to climb to the top of a firm, but they do want a chance to expand their knowledge, have diversity in their teams, and have accessibility to mentors.

The important part is to value the various skills that the different generations have in the firm and take advantage of what each can provide for the future. Businesses need both introverts and extroverts to fully succeed—this can help accounting firms address areas that they have not pursued previously and in the process tap into new opportunities with technology and social platforms.

The first thing that will attract the cloud generation is your firm having a clear purpose as a business. Accounting firms in the compliance era may have taken any client that came in the door, regardless of the segment they served. As the PwC report mentioned previously shows, millennials prefer to feel they have a mission they believe in that excites them about coming to work. Yes, cloud technology is attractive, but many of the ways that firms are currently structured are not.

Look at the traditional staffing model in a firm: entry level associate to senior associate to manager to senior manager to partner. The research shows that this model does not attract millennials. Many are not interested in becoming a partner or climbing a "corporate ladder." This generation doesn't want to work to just work or to try to attain a title—they want to ensure the work that they do gives them purpose.

We can change how firms attract new talent by bringing down the walls of how things used to be done. A collaborative culture can be created in which everyone works together as a team with a focus on rebuilding the client relationship. As we refocus our firms on what excites a new generation, we in essence, attract and groom cherished advisors of the future.

We can do this by combining talent and cloud technology together to create different industry segments within a practice, where you can specialize in certain industries or even certain service offerings under that umbrella. This way, you can broaden your offerings and have the opportunity to create client–accountant relationships that haven't existed in the majority of practices in almost a generation.

Millennials often approach collaboration from a different perspective than prior generations. They are much more comfortable working together and collaborating to accomplish a goal than doing it in a silo. I have children and family members in this age group, and I have witnessed this work dynamic up close. One time, my son and his cousin were playing the same game on their phones. They were sitting together, but not talking. My son got stuck at one point and couldn't get to the next level, so he turned to his cousin for help. With some guidance, he was able to move up to the next level and continue with the game.

Afterwards, I asked him if he felt he had accomplished the game's task. He said he had. When I was growing up, I would have never thought this way. If I didn't get to the next level by myself, I didn't feel a sense of accomplishment. But my son doesn't see things the same way as I did. The fact that he needed to consult with his cousin—and tap into his experience and insight—did not matter.

Another advantage of the millennial team building is that you can cultivate different expertise in different vertical niches. For example, your team for health and wellness clients may include different members than for your retail or nonprofit clients. This makes your teams more specialized in each particular industry, since the team's knowledge grows as they handle more and more clients within that segment. Your teams will begin to have benchmarks operationally and financially of other clients they deal with in the same space; this allows you to promote your firm as providing specialized experts in that particular industry, thus providing more value to your clients.

This vertical industry niche staffing approach also helps team members contribute their strengths to a larger effort, which helps improve efficiency and overall morale because he or she can see how their role supports the entire team and how it contributes to the larger effort of supporting the client. For instance, one member might be responsible for data entry, while another may oversee journal entry and coding. Another may manage cash flow and budget planning, while someone else fills the role of customer success manager, whose job it is to communicate with the client the findings and analysis of the team.

Standard Niche Team Roles

Each vertical-industry niche team had a bookkeeper, accountant, advisor, and customer success manager (CSM). If you don't have that many people working in your firm, one person may be doing more than one role: the business owner may be the CSM, and/or you may be outsourcing certain functions outside of your firm. See Figure 3.1 for an example of a typical collaborative staffing model.

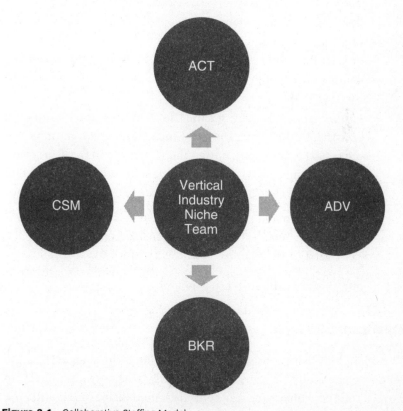

Figure 3.1 Collaborative Staffing Model

Here are the roles and what they do:

- *Bookkeeper (BKR)*. The bookkeeper ensures all the automated data flows properly between the accounting systems and any other applications, or the client's online banking. Imported transactions need to be checked for accounting accuracy and to ensure no duplication or transactions deleted. Transactions also have to be entered that were not automatically recorded by the systems. Any transactions that need to be sent or monitored for approvals by the client would be handled by the Bookkeeper as well.

- *Accountant (ACT)*. The accountant reviews the data for accuracy and proper presentation of the numbers. He or she will make any necessary journal entries and create a reporting package for the client.

- *Advisor (ADV)*. The advisor reviews what happened in the financials and interviews the clients to understand variances and make recommendations. He or she prepares budgeting or cash flow forecasting for the client and reviews supporting data to ensure they can keep the client on track throughout the year.

- *Customer success manager (CSM)*. The CSM takes the information prepared by the vertical industry niche team and communicates the results to the client. Rather than everyone in the firm speaking to a client, there is a team to prepare the data and collaborate and only one person who develops and nurtures the relationship. This way the client can receive individualized attention and not feel overwhelmed from having to communicate with a different person every time. The CSM also catches any issues in the relationship early on that he or she can solve and identifies other services the firm can offer, too.

Operations Team

The operations team consists of an information technology (IT) group, administrators, and partners. Rather than having each person set up new accounting files, you can centralize nonbillable work with the most qualified people. See Figure 3.2 for an example.

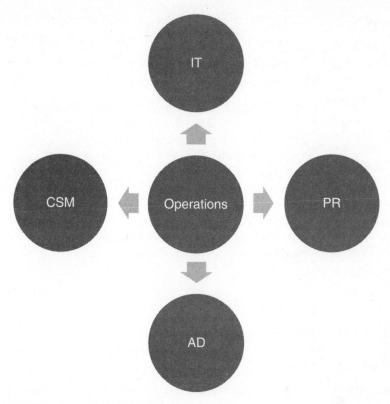

Figure 3.2 Operations Team Model

Here are the roles and what they do:

- *IT group (IT)*. The IT group creates new accounting files for clients, gets the integrations working, and ensures that all the reporting templates needed are in the file. Additionally, any tickets from the teams go through this group, and if the group can't answer the question, they centralize calling support from the various vendors being used, instead of everyone calling for support. This work can be outsourced if your firm doesn't have the budget to hire internally, as there are plenty of businesses that offer that support for a fee.

- *Administrators (AD)*. Administrators take client calls and provide duties like customer service, route support tickets, and monitor responses to close tickets. They are also responsible for firm reporting and general administration oversight.

■ *Partners (PR)*. Partners are the leaders of the practice. They review work and are responsible for business development and sales calls. They also oversee customer relationship management and overall operations.

Best of all, a vertical industry niche team approach offers millennials an opportunity to grow and expand. Rather than having to move up each year, they have the opportunity to move laterally within the same firm and learn about different vertical industry niches. It is also an opportunity to learn more about a new industry and gain knowledge of different technologies without having to leave the practice. This creates a more attractive recruiting tool for new talent and fits in the millennials' model for workplace satisfaction and continuous learning.

PRICING AND PACKAGING

Many accounting professionals still bill per hour. However, that is not a profitable approach for a cherished advisor team.

Charging by units can be traced back to the 1950s. During this time, the American Bar Association (ABA) was fearful that doctors' incomes were passing lawyers'. In response, the ABA published a pamphlet called *The 1958 Lawyer and His 1938 Dollar* (West Publishing Company, 1958), which suggested that the industry sell their services in units similar to mass production manufacturing—in this case by the hour.[2]

For the most part, it worked for accountants. It was easy to determine an accountant's worth by measuring how long it took to accomplish a specific task, and then to simply charge the client a specified rate based on those numbers of hours. Profits were measured in how many hours an accounting firm could accumulate and charge for.

Hourly rates are still a popular choice for billing compared with a flat fee. A survey conducted by the 2016–17 National Society of Accountants Income and Fees of Accountants and Tax Preparers in Public Practice Survey Report found that about one-third of firms bill by fixed fee (35.3 percent), hourly (31.2 percent), or a combination of the two (31.8 percent).[3]

But there are several flaws with the hourly approach.

During the past decades, global trade and technology have made it tough if not almost impossible for industries to make a profit in mass production that is driven by hourly rates. In addition, accounting software has made it easier and faster to do the basic accounting work, which means fewer hours to bill and thus less profit if billing by the hour. Just because technology has helped accountants do more work in less time does not mean the accountants' value has diminished.

The billable hour undercuts your value as an accountant and suggests that your services are interchangeable with others. If you step back and think about what is valuable to a client, it's the answer that you provide them in the form of advice or financial reports. If you get that answer in 10 hours versus 40 hours, it doesn't change the value of what you delivered. Actually, the client is happier because you provided them the answer in a shorter amount of time.

In the billable hour scenario, if you and another accounting firm offer the same services, the only difference from the client's perspective is how much time the works takes you and what is charged for the hours that are billed. If someone else is willing to charge less or do the same task in less time, they are deemed more valuable to the client because all they see are dollars and cents—and not your expertise and skills.

The other downside with the approach is that the client cannot see the accountant's value either. The client only receives a bill of hourly services, and does not see what it takes to accomplish that task—or why it may take that amount of time. This leaves clients frustrated because they do not know what an accountant's final bill may be until it arrives. So often they end up surprised by the total and cannot see why it took, say, 10 hours to complete a financial report. This also creates a bad experience for clients because they cannot budget for fees that may be charged to them.

In a *Journal of Accountancy* article called "The Firm of the Future," author Ron Baker argued that most businesses have prices and not hourly rates. Using the airline industry as an example, he pointed out that nobody would fly an airline that charges $4 per minute, because so many variables—seen and unseen—can cause the cost of your ticket to wildly vary. It's too unpredictable and thus creates a lack of confidence between the airline and the customer.[4]

Your advisory services can run into the same problem if you are not careful. A better way to bill for services—and one that helps both the accountant and the client—is to charge for packaged services.

Adam Davidson, writing in the *New York Times*, explained that companies like General Electric, Nike, and Apple long ago learned that the real value in their service to customers is not the end result, but rather the ideas that can transform their products far beyond their generic value. For example, Davidson writes, Apple doesn't want to be in the generic MP3-player business. There is too much competition and it is difficult for customers to see value in their MP3 compared with others. What makes their product so special? He says that Apple charges for the value in its MP3 product—that it offers more than the competitors and benefits the customers in more ways—not how long it takes to build, ship, and sell the product.[5]

Perhaps the greatest problem was that hourly billing motivates firms to focus only on long projects because they are more profitable, rather than those that required insight that couldn't be measured per hour. Also, the billable hour encourages accountants to spend more time than necessary on routine work rather than on the analysis clients need to run their business.

Cherished advisor teams correct this. They are created to offer a variety of services that can be billed in a more acceptable packaged base rate. The work within the team becomes repeatable and process-oriented, so that the right amount of time can be spent on the advisory side. As the teams get more knowledgeable and efficient, the work should take less time, and the advice should keep getting better. The clients can see exactly what that engagement entails and can budget for it, and the cherished advisor teams can devote their time and energy to producing value instead of focusing on tracking billable hours.

This pricing and packaging model of billing creates a win-win revenue model for you and your client. First, it builds a stronger one-on-one relationship with the client, which helps secure long-term contracts. Additionally, clients are happier because they know how much they are paying and are not afraid to receive the bill. It also strengthens your services. Billing by packaging services does not mean you charge less, but that you place a greater price on your overall value. It may take you and your cherished advisor team less time to perform certain tasks, but this means you have more time to do other work. You are working more like a mini-corporation that offers clients value—knowledge and financial expertise—rather than reports to meet a deadline without any explanation.

Let's say you have various flat fees that cover an outlined set of services. For instance, say you have a client in the health and wellness industry. You would charge $500 to do X, Y, and Z. This fee would cover your basic services, and then you could charge $600 or $700 per month to include additional services or to complete regular services more frequently or on a different time schedule. You can also adjust packaging of services for clients with different needs. Table 3.2 shows an example of what three packages may look like.

Table 3.2 Packaging Services

Package A	Package B	Package C
Quarterly reconciliation	Monthly reconciliation	Weekly reconciliation
Quarterly financials	Monthly financials	Weekly financials
Document collection and storage	Document collection and storage	Document collection and storage
Software training and support	Software training and support	Software training and support
Quarterly business analysis meeting	Monthly business analysis meeting	Biweekly business analysis meeting
	Accounting and expense management software	Accounting and expense management software
	Payroll reconciliation	Payroll reconciliation
		Multiple revenue stream reconciliation
		Multiple entity intercompany reconciliation
		Foreign exchange transactional analysis and review
		Bill pay collection and management

SUMMARY

The foundation for becoming a cherished advisor is how you develop and manage your relationship with your client. This interaction between accountants and clients goes beyond cloud technology, data, and figures—it is about delivering value that a client needs from an accounting professional, such that the client can't imagine not having you as part of the business. You establish this relationship by conducting in-depth interviews with the client to get a clear picture of the client's operations and accounting practices, as well as visiting with departments and employees to better educate yourself in all aspects of the business. From here, you identify the areas where you need more experience and education and then, by utilizing the growing and motivated millennial workforce, you create multiple-member teams to analyze the client's needs and then offer strategies and packaging services to best help your client's business meet its goals.

ENDNOTES

1. PricewaterhouseCoopers (PwC), *Millennials at Work: Reshaping the Workplace*, 2011, www.pwc.com/m1/en/services/consulting/documents/millennials-at-work.pdf.
2. Debra Cassens Weiss, "Accounting 'rogue outliers' seek to change billable hour." ABA Journal. Accessed August 07, 2017. http://www.abajournal.com/news/article/rogue_outliers_in_accounting_seek_to_change_billable_hour_said_to_be_promot/.
3. NSA Blogger, "NSA Survey Reveals Fee and Expense Data for Tax Accounting Firms in 2016 and 2017 Projections," National Society of Accountants MemberConnect, January 2017, accessed April 20, 2017, http://connect.nsacct.org/blogs/nsa-blogger/2017/01/27/nsa-survey-reveals-fee-and-expense-data-for-tax-accounting-firms-in-2016-and-2017-projections.
4. "Q&A: Should You Dump the Billable Hour?" *Journal of Accountancy*, February 2015, accessed April 20, 2017, www.journalofaccountancy.com/news/2015/feb/firm-billable-hours-201511763.html.
5. Adam Davidson, "What's an Idea Worth?" *New York Times*, July 29, 2013, accessed June 6, 2017, www.nytimes.com/2013/08/04/magazine/whats-an-idea-worth.html?mcubz=2.

CHAPTER 4

Strategies for Marketing Your New Advisory Experience

There is a famous saying: "You never get a second chance to make a first impression." That is true in every kind of relationship, but perhaps no more important than in how you present yourself to potential clients. If you do not make a strong initial impression, it is difficult to gain a client's interest or build trust when you try to convince him or her that you and your team offer the best advisory services for their business. If the client is not interested in you, then he or she will not be interested in your services.

Traditionally, when I ask accountants where their clients came from, most say from referrals and word of mouth. Accounting and bookkeeping practices are not always choosy about a potential client's industry; instead, they accept any industry because the services offered are more horizontal than vertical. This has been the accepted approach for decades. Much like law practices, many accountants do not promote or advertise their services because it feels uncomfortable and possibly "unprofessional." Accounting firms have been dependent on businesses with a certain mile radius from their office and word-of-mouth.

However, that approach is becoming extinct with the onset of the cloud and availability of potential clients anywhere in the country, or the world for that matter. You can no longer wait for business to come to you—you need to put yourself out there and grab it. Now with cloud technology and your vertical industry niche clientele, you can attract prospects based on your expertise and knowledge of their industry. This means you have to reinvent how you market your firm, your team, and your services.

Perhaps the greatest obstacle that accountants face with regard to marketing their services is their own mentality that they will be perceived as "selling" to their clients. That might sound strange—after all, who doesn't want to gain more clients and to be able to provide more services to their existing clients? However, many in the accounting industry don't want to push their services on a potential client for fear they would only sign on because of pressure, instead of an actual need for their accounting services.

As part of your transformation to advisory services, you need to change your mind-set about sales and marketing. Rather than feeling like you take advantage of your clients, or that you are selling them something they don't want or need, realize that a client will not hire you to perform services that he or she does not need.

HOW DO YOU WANT TO DESIGN THE CLIENT EXPERIENCE?

Your cherished advisory team cannot exist without customers, but before you reach out to a potential client, you need to create your client experience. This is often overlooked or taken for granted in a practice, but it is one of the most critical steps to get right in a client relationship. The client experience is defined as *interactions between a client and your practice throughout the entirety of the business relationship*. Interaction points to plan for on the journey can include awareness, discovery, relationship cultivation, advocacy, and service.

A strong customer experience has many far-reaching benefits for your business. A 2013 study by Oracle Global Research called "Global Insights on Succeeding in the Customer Experience Era" found that business executives estimated that the cost for not offering positive, consistent, brand-relevant customer experience is 20 percent of their annual revenue. Still, many businesses tend to underestimate the important of customer experience. Here are some other findings from that study:[1]

- 89 percent of customers say they have switched brands due to poor experiences.
- 86 percent of customers feel they are already paying for great customer experience.

This shows that how you create your customer experience can determine not only if you land an engagement, but also whether that client stays with you. This way, a client is able to see the value of your services, which justifies the rates you charge and any additional services you offer.

BUILDING AN OVERALL ARCHITECTURE

The best way to ensure a successful client experience—from initial contact through sales, marketing, and securing long-term relationships—is to design an overall customer-experience architecture. Think of this as the foundation from which your entire client relationship stands.

Your architecture is a blueprint for the actual journey you hope your client takes with you. You may have already found your vertical industry niche, built a strong and diversified internal team, and identified potential clients. However, before you set up a meeting to discuss a potential client's needs and what you can offer, you need your architecture in place. This not only helps you reestablish your team's goals and strengths, but helps to outline your credibility, define lines of communication, and demonstrate your potential value to clients.

There are many ways to design this architecture, and no one approach is right for everyone. However, this section describes a typical architecture that you can use as a guide when creating your own.

Your Mission Statement

Even if you have already created a mission statement, revisiting it can help clarify what your team can offer and why a client should be interested. Your team's mission statement should be one to two sentences in length and clearly state your business and brand's purpose. It doesn't need to be too specific or measurable, but it needs to explain your purpose for existing that can be clearly communicated and understood.

The statement should make reference to your long-term goals, take into consideration your brand's features and benefits, and target the right audiences. Successful mission statements share the following four elements:

Value
Why does your brand exist?

Inspiration
How do your goals inspire both employees and clients?

Plausibility

Is your goal reasonable, attainable, and realistic?

Specificity

Are you clear, not general, in describing your goal and purpose?

Don't mention your process and speak specifically about the company. Instead, focus solely on the benefits that your client, including its stakeholders and employees, will get from working with your practice.

Your mission statement should be a group effort. Meet with your team and ask questions to brainstorm key words. On a whiteboard, write all the words and phrases that come to everyone's mind. The more insight you have, the better. From this list, you can begin to build your mission statement around the key words your team comes up with. It may take time, and you will no doubt write multiple statements and several drafts of each before you narrow it down.

Here are some questions for you and your team to ask in order to help create your mission statement:

- Why do we exist?
- Whom do we serve?
- How do we do what we do?
- What are we really good at?
- What is unique about us?
- What is our driving force?
- What services do we offer?
- What needs do we satisfy?
- What market and region do we serve?
- Who are our ideal clients?

A sample mission statement might look like this:

> *We are a locally owned CPA firm that provides accounting, tax, and cloud advisory services to small businesses. We believe in a hands-on approach, being a strategic partner in your business and deploying best-in-class technology to serve you.*

Here are few other examples from some top accounting firms:[2]

KPMG LLP

"KPMG's mission is to turn knowledge and understanding of information, industries and business trends into value for our firms' clients, our people and the capital markets."

RSM McGladrey

"We will deliver global capabilities with the 'local' touch that brings world class assurance, tax and consulting expertise to our clients through enduring relationships built on genuine understanding and trust."

Kaufman Rossin

"Our philosophy is to provide knowledge and expertise—with unsurpassed dedication and sensitivity. We provide professional services to businesses and their leaders, offering experienced guidance at every stage of business growth."

EY

"To drive progress and make a difference by building a better working world—for our people, for our clients and for our communities."

CBIZ/Mayer Hoffman McCan

"Our mission is to help our clients prosper by providing them with a wide array of professional business and individual services, products, and solutions to help them better manage their finances and employees. We endeavor to provide superior client service and build long-term client relationships."

Your Brand Promise

Your *brand promise* (also referred to as *brand essence*) is what a potential client will get from your brand. In many ways, it is also a slogan for what your brand represents and the immediate image people have of your company or product. Keep your brand promise short, simple, credible, memorable, inspiring, and different.

Here are some examples of brand promises from various companies:

KLA-Tencor
"The yield company"

BMW
"The ultimate driving machine"

Xerox
"The digital document company"

Geico
"15 minutes or less can you save you 15% or more on car insurance."

Nike
"To bring inspiration and innovation to every athlete in the world"

Apple
"Think different."

Customer Experience

What do you want your client to *feel* during your interactions with your team and services? It is not about what they think of your work, but about the end result. For example, a restaurant wants customers to feel satisfied by food they otherwise would never make for themselves. An accountant's services are no different. Do you want your clients to feel relaxed from not having to deal with the stress of money management, or feel inspired to try new ways to expand their business?

Breaking Down Your Services into Segments

Most brands plan for the overall business, but often this can leave many loopholes. Instead, break down your business so your different services can be discrete units, such as budget planning, cash flow management, inventory oversight, and the like. Note anything that your team offers in terms of a service, no matter how small or seemingly insignificant. The goal is to identify each of the different services your team delivers to clients and what a client will experience as a result.

Creating Customer Segmentation

Every customer has a different set of expectations about your firm's brand. For instance, some may value convenience over price. Compare each segment of your services with the profiles of different customers, and define the needs of each of those personas—including the key drivers of their purchase decisions and their brand perceptions. The goal here is to match a potential client's needs to your services. What do you offer that lines up with those needs?

Brainstorm with your team to identify each segment's specific needs and how you can meet those needs, either by improving your existing processes and/or strategies based on your new findings or by developing brand new ones. While designing your experience, make sure it encompasses all the crucial factors, such as product and/or service, defined channels, content offerings, pricing and packaging, and client touch points.

Assessment and Deployment

Once you have put together the final draft of your customer-experience architecture, you should ensure that it is coherent and conveys integrity before you start publicizing it. Have some outside family members, friends, consultants, and/or clients provide feedback. As part of your final evaluation of this vitally important document, ask yourself these questions:

- Is the brand experience is expressed evenly across all platforms?
- Have all the discrete customer experiences been included in the overall architecture planning?
- Are the strategies enhancing or complementing other experiences?

HOW ACUITY DEVELOPED CLIENT INTERACTIONS

The following interview was conducted by Amy Vetter with Kenji Kuramoto, CEO and Founder of Acuity in Atlanta, Georgia.

What has been your biggest obstacle when it comes to client interaction and impression (making that initial connection with potential clients) with a vertical niche team? How did you identify it and overcome it?

Kuramoto: The biggest obstacle that we have faced has been remaining diligent in saying no to clients who do not fit within our vertical expertise because their business model doesn't match up with our industry specialty.

For example, recently a cannabis-based business out of California contacted our sales team and was interested in modernizing their accounting function by using our team. Regardless of individual beliefs as to whether this should be a legal business model at state and federal levels, we knew how quickly cannabis businesses were growing and I felt it worth taking on a new client in an industry we had never served to see if there were opportunities to help a developing group of entrepreneurs.

We signed the client and preceded to onboard them like any other new client. Then I started getting questions from our team about why we were working on this type of client and, more specifically, were there any concerns about the legality of serving a client in the cannabis industry. After researching this, we found that the State Boards of Accountancy in the states that our company operates had not specifically given clearance that serving cannabis-based business would not violate a CPA's requirement of "good moral character." In short, there was no guarantee that we weren't jeopardizing individual team member's CPA licenses.

Upon realizing this, I personally called this new client and explained that we couldn't serve them. So not only did I confuse and frustrate our own team, I had to turn a client away who we had led to believe that we could help—all because we weren't willing to stay within our own vertical expertise.

What did you find was the greatest challenge with initial client interaction? What did you learn, and what did you do to overcome?

Kuramoto: The most difficult challenge with initial client interaction is to establish trust. A business's financials are extremely personal to the business owner, so they are judging every bit of that initial interaction to look for signs of whether you can be trusted. Many of our sales team members are young in their careers and new to the profession, so they do not always have all of the answers a client's initial questions. We've had to learn how to do a better job of listening to the client, to ask questions to better understand their needs, and to be forthright in saying that while we may not know the answer to one of their questions right then, we will find it through one of our colleagues.

We believe that trust is not given to us by clients because we have all of the answers, but because we care enough about the client that we're going to go figure it out for them. We lost a lot of deals in the early days of our sales team by trying to sound smart, instead of showing empathy and a desire to help.

How did you create your marketing strategy? What did you decide to focus on, and what was your strategy for implementing?

Kuramoto: Our marketing strategy has been to build trust by giving up-front value to small businesses. We decided to focus on building content that business owners would find useful, specifically in the accounting and financial space, but often even in other areas that impacted entrepreneurs.

Our team developed most of the content, but we also interviewed other specialists like insurance brokers, attorneys, and investors. On our website, content lives in three main places. Our blog is updated with two pieces of content per week and can span anything from setting up your chart of accounts to how to raise venture capital. Our Stories page highlights one of our clients each month and seeks to provide content that our target market can really relate to by sharing the entrepreneurial journey our client has gone on to start their business. And our Resources page provides more specific tools to our audience that include e-books, infographics, and even calculators to help determine what their spend level should be on their accounting function.

What was your greatest marketing challenge, and how did you overcome it?

Kuramoto: In 2014, we began learning more and more about marketing automation tools that could deliver a sort of customized message to mass audiences. From a scalability perspective, that sounded like an amazing growth resource, so we decided to purchase marketing automation software and some lists of small business e-mails. We began using the software to send out e-mails to these lists but quickly started receiving spam complaints and angry replies. We did our best at the time to make our e-mails non-sales oriented and friendly, but we saw very few people interested in engaging with us in a positive way. What we soon realized is that while we had acquired a means to engage with an audience, we had not developed enough high-quality content that allowed us to spark a positive initial engagement with them and then cultivate that engagement over a requisite period of time. So by putting the engagement mechanism before the content creation, we wasted time, resources, and annoyed some prospects along the way. Not the way you want to start a marketing function!

CREATING AND IMPLEMENTING A MARKETING STRATEGY

If the idea of pursuing clients feels uncomfortable to you, the prospect of marketing your services may seem daunting as well. But marketing is essential for securing and maintaining client relationships. The more you can spread the word about your team and your services to your vertical niche client base, the more opportunity you have to separate yourself from the competition and attract the attention of potential customers.

The good news is that marketing today can be easy to implement and maintain. The Internet and social media channels have opened all kinds of pathways for accountants and bookkeepers to get their message out to the market. Marketing is another means to communicate your "why." Your first step is to design a marketing strategy and then to implement it through various marketing outlets.

Marketing Strategy

Your marketing strategy is one that combines all of your business's marketing goals into one comprehensive plan. It is based on the following three elements:

- Market research
- Business goals
- Service offering

Your fundamental goal with your marketing strategy is to increase revenues by attracting potential clients, retaining your existing customers, and providing upsell opportunities to other service lines. This approach can also help you sustain your competitive advantage.

Marketing Methods

Marketing today can take many forms, but while the Internet and social media have opened up new pathways for marketing, some of the tried-and-true methods still work. The main marketing methods you should explore with your team include the following:

Thought/Industry Leadership

This is an individual or group of people who are go-to authorities within your industry and the client's, who can help recognize trends and then implement strategies to achieve actual business results. You may reach out to these individuals or recruit them from within your team. For instance, team members may have more insight into social media trends or changes within a client's industry since they may interact with it on a regular basis.

Strategic Partnership

This is an arrangement between two companies or organizations to help each other, or work together, for a common purpose.

Referral Sources

You can promote your products or services to new clients by asking for referrals from companies in the same industry as your vertical niche.

Networking

You can (and should) reach out to individuals and associations in your vertical industry niche market. It's important to create personal connections to demonstrate that you are more than a business—you build a relationship. Taking time to invest in those relationships is important so that when prospects or leads come up in either of your networking circles, you are the first to think of each other and trust that the client will be handled well.

Event Hosting

Consider hosting organized get-togethers with local businesses in your vertical niche. For example, you might host casual lunches or after-work socials during which you offer some kind of "teaching" seminar for potential clients to learn more about you and your services.

You don't have to do all these, but this list gives you an idea of the types of marketing available. Which one (or ones) you choose depends on various factors, such as the budget you have put aside for marketing, your return on investment (ROI), and the ability to track engagement and success.

Internal Marketing

If your firm has several staff members or multiple departments, mining available opportunities internally can be just as important as external marketing. The benefit of networking internally is that you don't have to convince them you are the right accountant or bookkeeper for them. By meeting with tax professionals in other departments and educating them on the advisory services you offer, you can uncover needs within your own client base that may be good prospects for your service line.

Here are some ways that you can market internally:

Lunch-and-Learns

Schedule training sessions with associates and managers from around the firm to show them what you offer to clients. Visually providing examples of dashboards and different types of analysis your team can provide will give them a good feel for which of their clients are right for your services.

One-to-One Lunches

Schedule lunches with different associates and managers in your firm to educate each other on what you both do and how you can collaborate to uncover opportunities for each other in each of your books of business.

Weekly Team Meetings

Within your own team, there are opportunities to mine. Each team member is working on different clients and having his or her own conversations. By scheduling weekly meetings in which all team members go over the status of the clients they are working on and any opportunities they foresee within their client base, you can collaborate on proposing additional services. For instance, you may be providing bookkeeping services to a restaurant client. Through discussions with that client, you learn that the book-keeper is being asked questions that are more complex and geared toward the opportunity of opening another restaurant location. In a team meeting, this can be surfaced so that a strategy can be put together to offer this client virtual controllership or CFO services as well to prepare the analysis they need.

Staff Incentives

Build in incentive pay for staff members who either bring in new clients or upsell a current client into additional services. These rewards can help to drive the behavior of looking for new opportunities since your team is closest to the clients they are working with.

Marketing Budget

You can organize a solid marketing budget by following these three simple steps:

1. **Find your reliable revenue.**

    This is the minimum amount of money your company cur-rently makes each month. For example, if your company has revenue that ranges from $5,000 to $10,000 per month, the reli-able revenue is the lowest figure of $5,000. Any amount over that minimum is revenue that isn't recurring and can fluctu-ate from month to month. Next, subtract all monthly expenses from your reliable revenue, such as rent, payroll, and the like. Whatever is left over is the disposable income that is available for your marketing budget. Of course, you want to put aside money for unexpected costs and future growth initiatives, but this approach gives you an estimate of how much you have to work with.

Depending on your stage of business, you may not have clients or enough revenue to give you extra funding for marketing. Marketing is just as important, if not more, at this stage as well. You should consider your marketing investment as necessary as buying office furniture and equipment. In the beginning stages, your budget may be lower and you may have to draw from personal funds, make a personal loan to your business, or take out a loan from your bank. As long as you are aware of how these additional funds are going to be utilized, and your marketing decisions are not haphazard, it is worth the investment for the future growth of your practice.

2. **Determine where you want to invest your marketing funds.**

After you know the total amount available to spend on marketing, the next part is to organize how you intend to spend that investment. There are four factors that often influence how funds are spent: budget size, your past experiences, advice from outside marketing experts and consultants, and where you can reach your target clientele. Keep in mind that marketing efforts such as social media activities require that you invest your time. Others can be purchased for a minimal amount of money, such as small print advertisements in industry and trade publications in your chosen target market, website ads, and e-mail advertising.

3. **Make changes when needed.**

Budgets are never set in stone. You should evaluate and make adjustments in your marketing budget as you move forward and discover what works for promoting your cherished advisor services and what doesn't. You might need to invest more money into fewer marketing opportunities, or cut back spending in other ones.

Return on Investment

ROI is often tough to measure, because there is not always a direct correlation between the money you invest in your business and the revenue you receive. Your marketing efforts could come back in the form of new talent, an opportunity to interact with vertical industry niche prospects and clients in new ways, or an introduction into new software or other infrastructure that could help your business down the road. However, to the best of your ability, you should gauge your marketing efforts and have an idea of the intended outcomes you want from that investment. Here are some key concepts to keep in mind when figuring out your ROI:

Customer Acquisition Cost (CAC)

This is the total price needed to acquire a customer. You can estimate this cost by dividing the total costs associated with acquisition by the total number of new customers within a specific period.

Committed Monthly Recurring Revenue (CMRR)

This is the recurring revenue from your client. If you charge them the same amount each month for your services, that is your subscription revenue that you can use to evaluate the growth of your business.

Acquisition Cost Payback

This means the number of months of contribution margin to pay back the cost of acquiring a customer. It is calculated as shown here:

$$\text{CAC Payback Period} = \frac{\text{Total Sales \& Marketing Costs of Prior Quarter}}{\text{New CMRR Added in Prior Quarter} \times \text{Gross Margin \% of the Business}}$$

Value of Customer

There are two types of customer value: desired and perceived. Desired value is what customers want from your product or service. Perceived value is the benefit customers believe they get from a product or service after being purchased.

Acquisition versus Retention

As a general rule, getting regular clients to return and winning back lost customers is less expensive than acquiring new ones again and again.

Here is a simple formula that can help you calculate the ROI for marketing investment:

Total Value of New Clients Attracted

− (Cost of Marketing Materials + Staff Time Invested) = ROI

For example, if you invest $4,000 into marketing materials and $800 in paid staff time and attract $18,000 in new client business, your ROI would look like this:

($18,000 − ($4,000 + $800) = $13,200)/4,800 = 275% ROI

Marketing is also about networking. This can include things like going to networking events in your area, getting involved on boards and committees of associations, traveling to industry conferences, building your website, blogging, writing for industry publications, and engaging in all forms of social media.

ONLINE MARKETING

One advantage in this digital age is that there are many social media platforms where you can promote your services for free. It is almost a given that any serious company should have a presence across most social media outlets. One advantage of building a cherished advisor team is that you may have many members (or interns) with experience and interest in this area who can help establish your firm's social media presence.

This section describes how you can use social media tools to market your services.

Website

Your company website is the most essential part of your marketing architecture. All your other marketing efforts, no matter how successful, will be in vain if potential clients are driven to your website only to leave once they arrive.

In general, accountants can face several obstacles when it comes to public perception—fair or unfair. First off, many people are often afraid to contact an accountant because they feel intimidated. Many clients are experts at what they do but may not be very knowledgeable about accounting and finance, which can make them feel inadequate. They don't want to feel exposed when telling an accountant that they lack this knowledge. Your website is a way to break down that barrier and brush off the stereotypes of accountants wearing suits and ties and working on adding machines. Instead, create an approachable image so that prospects will be encouraged to contact you.

A website is a living, breathing thing—it's not something you set up once and never come back to. Your website should tell a story about the mission of your practice, the verticals you target, what your client experience is like, and who your team is. People do not look up companies in the Yellow Pages any more. They do their research on you before they make their first contact, including checking out your website in many cases.

Nowadays, basic website design has become a do-it-yourself endeavor. There are many free website templates available, as well as services that show you how to design your own website, but remember that your team members are accountants—not designers. Just as your clients need an accountant to do their finances, you should hire an expert to design your website. It is worth the investment; this is your "storefront," so don't skimp on costs for quality.

The big problem with free templates is that it's too easy to use the same template as another accounting firm and/or display the same stock images. If you look like everyone else, it's impossible to stand out or communicate a differentiated message.

A website is a reflection of who you are as an accounting or bookkeeping practice. It is also an opportunity to introduce yourself and your team in a more personal and appealing way. Use your website to feature stories of the individuals who make up the business. For instance, you could showcase your own and your team members' interests besides accounting. Does anyone surf or hike? Show pictures of them enjoying one of their favorite beaches or trails, so you can connect with clients and prospects who have the same interests.

Your website should be kept up-to-date, preferably every day if possible, with new content and valuable resources for your clients to always refer back to. Your website designer will work with you to outline your website's look, feel, and content to make sure that it meets your business goals and attracts the vertical industry niche clients you want. For instance, if you are targeting restaurants, allow the design to reflect key elements of that industry. Rather than just listing prices, you can design it like a restaurant menu and show your packages in a format that resonates with the clients you are trying to attract.

Here is a summary of certain characteristics your website needs to have to garnish sufficient attention from visitors:

Headline or Tagline

A headline is derived from your mission statement and becomes the tagline for your practice. It is often the first information visitors see, so it needs to grab their attention and communicate who you are and what you do in a brief, concise manner. Otherwise, the visitor will just move on.

Lead Capture

You can acquire e-mail addresses from potential clients by offering content in exchange for giving an e-mail address. With these e-mail addresses, you can then use an autoresponder to reach visitors and explain more about your services.

Testimonials

As with LinkedIn, adding testimonials can offer instant credibility. Place a testimonial on each page, if possible, and make sure to identify who it came from and his or her company. Don't make the testimonials sound the same; try to have each one highlight a different aspect of your services, if possible, such as customer service or an improved business outcome. Your clients are often more than happy to offer testimonials so reach out them.

Client Portal

Create an exclusive, secure area on your website for clients to upload documents and communicate with you. You can also get personalized content for your clients or have exclusive resources that the general public wouldn't receive—an added value for being a client of your practice.

Navigation

Having a simple table of content can further help keep someone on your website. A confusing layout or hard-to-read fonts will frustrate visitors and push them away. Keep the navigation simple and easy to follow—no more than four to seven tabs at the top or on the side.

Call to Action

Highlight a *call to action* on the page, such as downloading a PDF that summarizes your services, viewing a video, or requesting a consult.

Social Shares

While obsessively posting on social media can be a waste of time, when you do write an article, update your blog, or want to promote an industry-related news item, make sure to post the link from your website and share it across all your social media platforms so people come back to your site to view it. Other people who then share your content also can help contribute to a high search engine ranking.

Content

People want go to websites for information—this can be information that is standalone and never changes as well as new content that is posted on a regular basis. If people know you offer new content, they are more likely to revisit. If you or no one on your team is a skilled writer, you can hire someone to help you pen articles and blogs. Begin with posting new content at least weekly, and make sure that the information is relevant to your business, services, and objectives.

Social Media

Social media outlets like LinkedIn, Twitter, Facebook, and YouTube are ideal platforms to implement your marketing strategy, as they can reach thousands if not millions of people and businesses and can help you engage with many other people and companies within your vertical niche.

Social media is always changing and evolving. It's a fast-paced approach to marketing and communication, so it needs regular attention and engagement. Your commitment to social media can be quite valuable, but you need to make sure that you are properly set up to take advantage of what it can offer and that you enlist the right people and personnel to manage it on a daily basis.

The social media outlets mentioned above are the primary ones that companies can best utilize and they are still the most popular. As you go along, you may discover that certain social media works better than others and you may want to adjust your strategy to devote more time to them and less to others.

Also, keep in mind that you don't have to be involved with every type of social media out there. For instance, Tumblr, Instagram, and Pinterest are oriented toward more visual posts. These work well for business that have a "visual" product (food, manufacturing, etc.), but may not be ideal for you, depending on who you are trying to attract.

Here is a closer look at the big four—LinkedIn, Facebook, Twitter, and YouTube—and how they may benefit your marketing efforts to promote your services and find potential clients.

LinkedIn

This is considered the "professional" social medial outlet and is ideal for posting news about your company and industry and recruiting potential new clients. Join LinkedIn Groups for your industry niche. If you want to draw people to your website, you can post a partial article on LinkedIn, and add a link to your website where the full article is posted.

Here are some other ways to strengthen your presence in LinkedIn:

Use Search and InMail

You can expand your connection by searching for people who have certain titles and/or businesses of a specific size. For example, you can search for a term like "CEO at companies with 1–10 employees." LinkedIn offers a way to message them to ask for a connection or inquire about their business.

Check Your Connections

Sometimes people in your connections change jobs that could benefit you. Periodically review your network and look for updates.

You can also sign up for e-mail announcements that can alert you to job changes or promotions.

Post Status Updates to the LinkedIn Social Network

LinkedIn allows you to post status updates either solely to your connections or publicly. Post helpful articles or website links to informative content that drives people to your website. You can also post published articles from trade publications or your company's blog (described in the "Blogging" section later in this chapter) to LinkedIn Pulse, the company's publishing platform. Followers received instant notification of your article, which can further boost your profile and provide news about your company as well as help drive traffic to your website. Also, your posts will be search-engine friendly, which can help potential clients find your company when searching for certain subjects and key words.

Add Video to Your Profile

In your biography, add a summary of your expertise, and, if possible a video. If you want people to get a feel for your personality and who you are, this is a great way to do it.

Add Testimonials

Testimonials can bring credibility to your services. List them in your summary, which can be more easily seen by potential clients. Need testimonials? Ask your connections with whom you have worked—and offer to return the favor.

Add Links to Your Profile

Add links to your website and even company contact e-mails.

Create a Company Profile Page

Your company profile is like a mini-website where you can showcase your services and what you can offer clients. LinkedIn can walk you through the process, but here are the main areas you need to focus on:

- *Your business name.* Make sure it reads the same as in your profile. For example, add LLC or Inc. if that's in your official business name.

- *Logo*. You can upload a standard company logo.

- *Company description*. Describe who you are and what your business does—and most importantly, where you want to go.

- *Specialties*. You have about 250 characters (about two- or three-word descriptions) to mention key services you want to highlight.

- *Twitter and company blog URL*. Adding these can help keep your page active.

- *Company type, size, and URL*. You are given the option to select your type of business and size. Your company website link can direct visitors to your home page or to a specific page that highlights or summarized your services.

Check out the company pages of companies like Google, AppleOne, Coca-Cola, Four Seasons Hotels and Resorts, BlackRock, and Evernote for inspiration.

Facebook

A Facebook business page gives you the ability to create specific private group pages within Facebook, and offers additional advertising opportunities to reach different clients. For example:

Targeted Facebook Ads

You can upload client e-mail addresses and Facebook will find people like those contacts, to whom you can send advertisements. You also have the option to send ads to certain community pages that your potential clients might follow.

Fan Pages

There is almost every kind of fan page for almost every kind of interest. The people who follow those pages can be potential clients. Also, join private groups that complement your niche industry.

Twitter

Twitter is still a great vehicle for promoting your services. However, you don't want all or your tweets to push your business. For every tweet you create about your company, develop four that are value-driven and educational about your industry or the latest news. You can increase your followers by following other people and businesses in your industry. Many will return the favor and follow you back. Here are some other tips to help you get the most out of Twitter marketing:

Run Twitter Ads

Twitter ads are an inexpensive way to reach more people by targeting certain locations, followers, or accounts.

Search for Hashtags

Hashtags (e.g., #accounting #advisors, etc.) can help your tweets reach larger audiences and target specific markets by joining a larger group of tweets. You can search for relevant hashtags through Twitter as well as checking out hashtags.org.

Stay Engaged

The key to Twitter success (and Facebook too) is regular engagement. Engagement is not only when you post new content, but also when you "retweet" to your followers or "like" other content or posts by people or companies you follow. You can also add comments about theses posts and open a dialogue between you and others Twitter users. Engagement can help keep people in your industry niche informed about you and your services as well as open the door to new introductions. However, to take full advantage, you need someone to not only post on a regular basis, but to also monitor your Twitter for updates and trends. This can be someone from your team, or you can outsource a social media consultant to oversee all social media content, posting, engagement, and activity reports, which are a weekly summary of your social media traffic and feedback that can help identify certain how certain content is working.

YouTube

Just like a blog post or an e-mail, a YouTube channel can be a great source of leads and traffic; however, it does require more time and consistent action to get the best results. Still, this can be a great way to highlight your team and services when you give a presentation. It is also a creative outlet to show the "fun" side of your business. As with your website, you could conduct "behind-the-scenes" interviews with team members about their hobbies and interests. The New York–based firm WithhumSmith + Brown has used their popular YouTube channel to showcase their flash mobs announcing annual meetings and comedy skits that help break through accounting stereotypes. They have fun with their profession, and it makes them look like a firm that would be fun to do business with.

Blogging

Blogging is an effective way to reach out and communicate with clients and potential customers. It can also further enhance your business's brand awareness, and market your services to a larger audience.

A blog can improve your firm's image as well as help drive more traffic to your website. Specifically, blogging can help your firm to:

- Stay connected with your current clients
- Educate potential customers about your services
- Showcase your team's expertise and knowledge
- Enhance your website's search engine rankings
- Create another platform for all your social media
- Reach out to prospects with whom you cannot connect through traditional sales and marketing

There are many free blogging services you can use, including Squarespace, Blogger, and WordPress. However, it's best to add your blog to your website, as it can help bring in more traffic.

Many web-hosting companies offer free blogging tools, but some charge a small fee. Your blog will become a part of your website with its own address, for example: www.websitename.com/blog.

For the best results, you do need to invest time into making your blog current and relevant to visitors. You might need to hire a writer to help you pen your blog posts if your team does not have the writing skills, or an editor to help edit their writing. You can also reach out to other related industry blogs to "share" stories: posting their stories on your blog with links back to the original articles. This can help you build content and address different topic areas.

No matter who writes your blog posts, there are certain areas that always need to be addressed. Here are some tips:

■ *Stick to what you know.* You're an accountant, so stick to your areas of expertise. Don't write about what you don't know or about personal topics.

■ *Add value.* Give readers helpful, useful, and timely accounting or bookkeeping information.

■ *Involve your team.* Encourage your members to contribute as much as possible. This will make your business appear more personal as well as more knowledgeable.

■ *Write for a regular audience.* Avoid technical writing and unnecessary accounting jargon that readers may not understand. Keep the language simple, conversational, and most of all interesting. Give them some kind of takeaway value with every blog post.

■ *Understand your audience—and empathize.* Explain how your expertise can directly benefit your potential client. Talk to them in *their* business language, not yours.

■ *Keep it short, but not too short.* Most blog posts are between 400 and 800 words. Posts that are shorter than that will be ignored by search engines. If the posts are too long, however, you may lose a reader's attention. One option: divide a post into two parts that you post on different days.

■ *Make blogs appealing.* Make blogs visually appealing with subheads and easier to read with bullet points. Add charts and graphics when possible. "How to" videos are also helpful.

■ *Maintain momentum.* Update, update, update. Nothing will kill a reader's interest more quickly than blogs that are not updated on a regular basis. If they like what you write, they will want to read more, so give them what they want. This doesn't mean you must write a new post every day, but set up a schedule and stick with it, like once a week at first and then twice a week after that. Post on the same day(s) too, so readers won't have to guess when the next post will be out.

Once you have written a blog post, you need to distribute it through your e-mail list of clients and website visitors who have shared their e-mail addresses, as well as across all social media platforms. Consider adding social media buttons to your posts, too; that way, people will be able to share your content easily, bringing in more readers.

E-mail Newsletters

As with your website content and blog, a weekly e-mail newsletter can help both you and you clients. However, many newsletters fail because they are not sent out on a regular basis and/or the content is bland and misguided.

Your newsletter should offer something for the reader/subscriber. Make the content informative and personal. For example, you can highlight a news story that is related to their industry, or changes in tax laws or other financial information that could affect their business. You can send a condensed version of your most recent blog, or profile one of your team members. The more valuable content you can provide to small businesses owners, the more you can seed a relationship of trust with them that may allow you to ultimately serve them as a client.

Distributing your newsletter through e-mail marketing services such as MailChimp, Constant Contact, AWeber, GetResponse, and ActiveCampaign can help you track how many people actually open the newsletter attachment so you can gauge interest.

E-mail Signatures

Creating a unique e-mail signature can be a simple way to promote new social media and website content, or new services. For example, a signature might include a phrase or question that links to your blog or other website content, like "Do you make these five cash flow mistakes?" It's another way to promote and market your services and expertise to both existing and potential clients.

NETWORKING

Your networking never ends. You should always work at exposing your brand and services to new and even existing industries. The more seeds you plant, the better chance you have of one of them bearing fruit. Here are some suggestions on how you can keep up your networking efforts:

Local Chamber of Commerce Meetings

Attending Chamber of Commerce meetings is a great way to meet local businesses, learn more about your community, and begin building referrals.

Meetup Groups

Meetup.com is a website where you can host a local gathering around a specific topic. Odds are your market already has a meetup in your area you could join, but if they don't, use it as an opportunity to begin one.

Vertical Industry Niche Conferences

Not only are conferences great opportunities to meet potential clients, you gain the chance to learn more about the industry (and the problems they face). You can also invest in a hosting a booth to further promote your services, or better yet be a sponsor or speaker at the conference. When you set yourself up as an expert, you build credibility and will be the one that those prospects think of when they are looking for an accountant or bookkeeper.

Industry Associations

Target associations related to your vertical niche. For example, if restaurants are potential clients, join the National Restaurant Association or its state chapters. As with attending industry conferences, you can expand your knowledge about issues and changing trends. But don't stop with regular memberships. Get involved and join boards and committees so they see you as involved and helping them succeed. As more people get to know you in the organization for your contributions, natural referrals will come.

REFERRALS

Offer your clients an incentive to bring in new clients. For example, a discount for a service or a small token of appreciation like gift cards to a restaurant or a movie theater. Make sure to promote this incentive through your social media accounts and in your newsletters.

SUMMARY

Accounting and bookkeeping practices were not always choosy about a potential client's industry; instead, they accepted clients from any industry because services that were offered were more horizontal than vertical. Much like law practices, many accountants did not promote or advertise their services because it felt uncomfortable and possibly "unprofessional." Accountants were dependent on businesses with a certain mile radius from their office or who heard of the company through word-of-mouth.

That approach is quickly becoming extinct with the onset of the cloud and availability of potential clients anywhere in the country, or the world for that matter. You can no longer wait for business to come to you—you need to put yourself out there and grab it. This means you have to reinvent how you market your firm, your team, and your services.

By focusing your attention and resources on internal aspects such as mission statements and brand promises, you can build an overall client experience architecture and then create and implement a marketing strategy that emphasizes website infrastructure, social media engagement, and networking opportunities to attract potential vertical industry niche clients.

ENDNOTES

1. *"Global Insights on Succeeding in the Customer Experience Era."* Report. 2013. Accessed August 7, 2017. http://www.oracle.com/us/global-cx-study-2240276.pdf.
2. "Accounting Mission Statements," MISSIONSTATEMENTS.com, May 2017, accessed June 8, 2017, www.missionstatements.com/accounting_mission_statements.html.

CHAPTER **5**

Creating a Successful Sales Model and Client Onboarding Process

You have built a client experience architecture, designed and implemented a marketing strategy, and even increased your networking efforts to attract potential vertical industry niche clients. What happens when you gain the attention and interest of a possible client? That is when you need to put on your sales hat and make your pitch for their business.

Accountants often view the word "sales" as a bad word—but the reality is that sales skills are also the greatest need for building your cherished advisor practice.

Traditionally, accountants, by nature, are not in the business of selling their services. They never had to go out and get clients, but rather relied on customers to come to them by word-of-mouth. But in this new technology age, potential clients are outside of your 10-mile radius, so learning how to sell your services becomes increasingly important. You not only need to make connections with potential clients through your marketing efforts, social media engagement, and industry networking, but when you do make that connection, you need to show why you are valuable to a client through all the wonderful services you offer that can help to improve their lives.

THE SCIENCE OF THE SALE

Typically, the topic of selling is uncomfortable for accountants. I have found that one of the main issues accountants face with the idea of selling is that they believe they may be taking advantage of the client if the client signs on for additional services—instead of believing the client not only wants their services, but also wants to pay for them. Others can feel it doesn't seem appropriate for a "professional accountant" to be a salesperson. The fact is, selling is a skill that is not spoken about as you move through your career; therefore, the foundation for putting the right skills in place is missing by the time you are responsible for bringing in clients.

Selling is connecting a need or pain point to the value you bring to a client. Keep in mind that your services are viewed as valuable to clients and they are looking to purchase those services. If they don't purchase the services from you, they will from someone else. As an advisor, you help businesses to grow and expand so the client can become more profitable; it is important that these services are offered by people like you, and paid for by clients, so that more clients can live their dreams of prospering rather than going out of business too soon.

Because of a lack of training in selling, an obstacle can be that the sales process seems ambiguous and is not a skill. But, the reality is that a good sales model is not about creating something new every time, but following a specific, proven process. You may have heard sales referred to as an "art," and yes, some individuals can make it look easy and effortless, but there is a science behind selling—and it is not that complex to understand and follow. Anyone can become good at selling with a basic understanding of how the process works.

Some may conjure up an image of a car salesman when the term *sales* is used and think a salesperson has to be pushy and forceful to succeed. Actually, a sale is a collaborative and consultative effort between you, your team, and the client. Your potential clients are already knowledgeable in many ways about what they need help with. Your job is not necessarily to tell them what they need, but instead educate them on the services you offer that fulfill their business needs.

When you change your mind-set about what sales involves and what areas you need to focus on, you will find the entire process much easier to implement.

THE SIMPLE SALES PROCESS

In the prior chapters of this book, we have discussed how to define your target client by selecting industries that you want to focus on. Additionally, we have gone over marketing techniques to attract the clients that you want. The sales process begins once the potential clients you have targeted contact you. Keep in mind that sales does not need to be complex. The process can be broken down into three categories:

- Discovery and qualification
- Client presentation
- Engagement letter

Discovery and Qualification

In this phase, you will accumulate information from the prospect in order to design your formal presentation as well as qualify him or her to determine if you both are a good match. Just because a client contacts you does not mean that he or she is a good fit for you—or that you should automatically take him or her as a customer, even if there is the potential for a lucrative contract. The sales process cannot only help the client understand if you are a good fit, but also help you gauge whether the client relationship will be a fit for you practice as well.

The discovery phase begins once a potential client has contacted you and you set up a time to meet (preferably face-to-face, in person or by video conferencing). For this initial meeting, you want to prepare a list of "discovery" questions to ask. The focus here is about research and exploration—and not about selling or explaining your specific services just yet. You want to gather all the information about the client's business, accounting practices, and issues so you can present an in-depth presentation that address their needs. Make sure that the client knows the agenda for this initial meeting and what you are hoping to get out of it. Another option is to provide prospective clients with a client interview checklist upfront so they can come prepared to your first meeting and have an idea of the questions you will be asking.

After the discovery interview, you should know at least the following key areas:

- The client's budget for your accounting services
- How the client currently manages finances—his or her current accounting systems (and what the client likes/dislikes about it)
- The client's problems, challenges, and dissatisfactions—his or her "pain points" with the way things are done today
- The client's short and long-term goals
- The time frame for the decision-making process on choosing an advisory service
- All the players involved in the decision making process
- Your competitors in the proposal process

The discovery questions help both you and the client. The investment during the discovery phase can go a long way to ensuring you secure the relationship, but it also helps as a great reference later when the prospect becomes your client to ensure you are delivering what you both initially intended. Devote enough time to prepare questions and then share them with your team for feedback. According to Shelley F. Hall, principal of Catalytic Management, LLC, great discovery questions can do the following:[1]

- Help the prospect see problems or challenges he or she didn't realize existed, which broadens your possible solution
- Frames the conversation around solutions and creates the image that your company solves problems, not just pushes product/services
- Determines how to customize your service/product presentation by focusing on the benefits and solutions that are the most relevant and most important to the customer
- Establishes your team's credibility by demonstrating your understanding of the prospect's industry or market
- Provides an opportunity to assess the prospect's buying and communication style so presentations and proposals are targeted to how the prospect wishes to receive and process information
- Uncovers the decision criteria and decision makers (those who need to receive the information about your services)
- Gives you a glimpse of the potential objections and gives you the opportunity to answer those objections early in the conversation
- Explores the value and/or importance of solving the prospect's problems

Creating Discovery Questions

You can only get the information you need by asking good questions. Rarely will clients offer you the insight and details you want. However, by asking good questions, you will get even better answers. Here are the type of questions you can consider asking.

Open-Ended Questions

Make sure every question is open-ended so the client is encouraged to talk and share. Business people enjoy talking about their business, so let them. Here are some basic open-ended questions to begin with:

- How would you describe your business?
- What kind of customers do you target? Why?
- What about your business, if anything, keeps you up at night?
- What are your short- and long-term goals for your business?
- What systems do you currently use?
- What do you like and/or not like about your current systems?
- In a perfect world, what would your systems do and tell you on a daily, weekly, and monthly basis?
- Why are you looking for an accounting professional?
- What are you looking for in an accounting professional?
- What, if anything, went wrong in your previous dealings with an accounting professional or consultant?

Layering and Probing Questions

The purpose of layering and probing questions is to find out what customers mean by what they say. You must understand exactly what is going on in the customer's mind and not make assumptions about anything. Layering and probing questions must be open-ended to be effective. Use them throughout the discovery interaction. This information will help you customize your presentation so the customer becomes excited about your process. For example:

- Can you tell me more about...?
- What did you mean when you said...?
- How so?
- What does that mean to you?
- Why is that?
- Can you elaborate on...?

- Can you clarify what you meant by...?
- What did you mean by...?
- What are your thoughts on...?
- Can you define...?
- Why is that important...?
- What are your ideas on...?
- Can you give me an example of...?
- How does that look to you?
- Can you say more about...?

Keep in mind that you may have to return for another discovery interview if you find you need more information. Don't feel badly if you have to do this. After all, the more information you can gather, the better you can help your client.

Qualifying Review

As you go through the discovery phase, you also are qualifying the client to determine if they are a good fit for your team as well. The answers they provide and how they present the information can help you gauge whether there are any personality conflicts or other potential red flags. Remember: You want to work with this prospect, but even if the business is in the right vertical industry niche and has the potential to be a lucrative client, if the prospect does not complement your goals and ways of doing business, you will eventually run into problems.

To define your "ideal" client so that you have the profile you want for your clients, you and your team should do the following:

- Define client(s) you work with that are the ideal clients and describe why. What makes them great to work with?
- What are your ideal client's typical needs?
- Define the worst client(s) you have had and why. What broke down the relationship or caused friction?

Make sure they are the type of organization that you want to work with and that shares similar values to yours. You want to learn all about the client company, culture, and values. It is better to step away now during the discovery phase than down the road after you have begun a relationship. When asking potential questions to determine whether this prospect would be a good fit for your practice, consider the following questions:

- What are the priorities the prospect is working on, and where do you fit in? Do you have to change your business platform too much to meet the client's demands? For example, your vertical industry niche may be in the nonprofit industry, but your new client may be in the automotive industry. If you have to alter too much of your team's approach in terms of technology, processes, services and support, it may be too costly and burdensome for you to take on that client.

- What is the prospective client's motivation for looking for accounting or advisory services? Does the client value accountants? How many accountants has the company gone through and why did they break it off? Was it because the accountant was not offering the quality of service they wanted (for example, not returning calls), or did the client not value what the accountants offered (for instance, saying they were too expensive)?

- How do the prospect's representatives treat other members of their staff, and how are the interactions between you and them? How people treat others is a good insight into how they will treat you and your team members. Talent is hard to find, so if a client is not aligned with your values as a firm, it can be a risk to take that client on. Ensuring you provide guidance on your values and how you treat staff and how you expect your clients to interact with your team is important so that you retain your employees.

After you have defined your ideal client, you will have a profile or persona to which you can compare a prospect once you complete your client interview. You can even create a "report card" of sorts and rate your prospect against this profile as A, B, C, D, or F to determine whether it's worth it to take next steps. Determining a good or a bad client early saves you time, frustration, and potentially money early on. Don't be afraid to turn down the wrong opportunities for your practice so that you can fill your practice with the right type of clients.

Discovery Exercise

Asking questions sounds simple, but it does take some level of preparation and practice. They say practice makes perfect and that is definitely true when it comes to sales. For some, sales may come naturally, but for many accountants working to perfect your skills can help your success rate in closing new clients.

Since sales is about asking questions, listening, problem-solving, and personal interactions, work on all of these as much as possible before your client presentations with your co-workers, family, or friends. Eventually, you will discover your strengths and weaknesses and can adjust what you practice to hone in more on the areas that need the most attention.

A good way to practice the discovery phase is to try several dry runs where you practice gathering information on a potential client. Practicing will help get over any nervousness and fine-tune your people skills so you appear more approachable and friendly. Going through a possible client scenario as a team exercise also can help get everyone involved so they all can work on their skills as well as provide feedback on areas of improvement.

You can ask another business you may have connected with through your networking to act as a test business to whom you can ask discovery questions. You can also create a mock situation with your partners, co-workers, or friends to role-play and practice. Another way is to go through the process with a "sample" company.

You can use an existing client of your own and pretend they are a prospect, a potential client you have researched that you would want as a prospect, or an actual prospect that you will be meeting with.

The goal of the exercise is to examine the information you want to collect from the client and work with your team to see if there is other information that may be missing—or that you need more detail about. Doing this can help you learn how to ask the next level of layering questions during the discovery process. At a minimum, ask each team member to write down three questions they would want to ask that client, based on your limited information on that client and what you know to be your ideal client.

This will give you a good start to get the exercise going. Take turns, then create layering questions to ask during follow-ups, like if you need additional information from the client, so you can properly prepare your presentation. Try this with your team and see what kind of additional questioning they come up with.

Client Presentation

The formal client presentation is when you take what you have learned during the discovery process and match it with your services for the potential client. During the presentation, you are not "selling" your company, but rather addressing the "pain points" the prospect is having—and then offering solutions through your specific services (i.e., how you can fix the problem).

This is also when you can introduce pricing and which of your packages fits best with their budget that they shared during the discovery interview. When you present this, it is always good to offer three options with the different services described to show why the pricing is different between them. This way, your client can see what you can offer to fit their initial budget, but also to see what additional services they could get for an additional fee. Even if they cannot afford the higher priced packages right now, it allows them to see what is available and how their business may benefit by making an additional investment in your services down the road.

The key to effective presentations is coming back to how you effectively communicate connecting your value to their needs. Besides the information you prepare, taking time to focus on *how* you present that information through your communication skills, expressions, and body language is also important.

As you get ready for your client presentation, keep in mind that your how you say it sometimes is more important than what you say in terms of making a first impression. Remember prospects and clients need to know, like, and trust you to put their business in your hands. Always devote serious thought to what you want to ask and present rather than "winging it." Think "why do they need me?" to project a credible attitude. Here are some other suggestions for an effective sales meeting presentation, from Phyllis Weiss Haserot, author of *The Marketer's Handbook of Tips & Checklists*:[2]

Attitude

- Nonverbal cues garner 90 percent of the attention.
- Come across as likeable, someone they would like to spend time with. Smile.
- Show through passion a belief in your message and what you are selling.
- Don't appear defensive, whatever they may question.

Credibility

- Factors that convey credibility include:
    - Perception of honesty and commitment
    - Sincerity of interest in helping
    - Perception of education, knowledge, and experience
    - Dynamic delivery
- These aspects of language detract from credibility:
    - Hesitation; voice fading
    - Ending statements with a questioning voice tone
    - Hedging
    - Overdoing "very" and other intensifiers
    - Compound questions
    - Tentative words like "hopefully"
    - Absolute terms like "never" and "always," unless documented

Engagement Letter

If your presentation was successful and the client decides to select you, then you can move to the next phase: drafting an engagement letter. An engagement letter is the contract between the client and accountant that defines scope of work and the responsibilities and obligations of each of the respective parties. It offers two main objectives:

- Offer important defense against a malpractice cause of action.
- Outline the specific scope of services rendered, including payment terms, retainers, expenses, and additional fees.

Speak with an attorney to set up your engagement letter that reflects the laws of your state. In terms of time frame, arrange the letter to cover one year of services. This gives both parties ample time to work together to determine whether they both want to continue the relationship. Another advantage of annual agreements is that it gives your client an opportunity to perhaps add additional services you provide once they see the results of your partnership, and also provide an opportunity for you to raise your rates, if needed, or elect to not continue with a client.

Another good practice is to add in a 90-day clause for a new client to review the engagement letter and ensure the scope that was outlined originally was accurate. Many times, once you begin with a client, you find that the scope of work was missing key things that you were not made aware of during the discovery phase. This clause allows you the opportunity to have a discussion with the client after the first 90 days to determine whether fees and scope need to be adjusted.

Besides outlining in detail with clear language the scope of your relationship and the specific services you will offer, an engagement letter also protects you from early termination on the client's behalf. Additionally, if you want to end the relationship before the year is up, you can include a clause around that too. For instance, if the client suddenly wants to terminate the agreement, you could have a clause that 30 or 60 days' notice is required in writing. This way you have some cash flow protection and transition planning.

Engagement letters also can help protect your team. Recruiting, hiring, and training new employees is an expensive endeavor, and you should be compensated for losing a key team member if a client decides to recruit him or her. My remedy for this has been to include a clause in my engagement letters that hiring away a member of my team requires a "recruitment" fee of 50 percent of that person's annual salary. Thankfully, I have never had to enforced this policy, but it did create a good business conversation the few times this occurred to discuss what the future relationship would be like if they decided to pursue that path.

Engagement Letter Checklist

In an article for the *Journal of Accountancy*, John F. Raspante, CPA, and Stephen Vono provided the following checklist of things you should consider including in an engagement letter:[3]

- *Exclusion clause.* Because accounting and advisory services can be broad, an exclusion clause that identifies what services will *not* be provided can be invaluable. For example, a payroll tax preparation engagement might exclude independent contractor classifications, labor regulations, ERISA (Employee Retirement Income Security Act) compliance, and the reasonableness of officers' compensation.

- *Deadline for submitting client information.* It is essential to establish a date by which the client must provide information needed each month, quarter, or year to prepare the accounting.

- *Stop-work provisions.* Although stop-work provisions are typically used for nonpayment of fees, you can consider them for conflicts of interest or for clients who provide accounting information late, refuse to take the advice, or act unethically.

- *Limitation on use of the accounting information.* Clients may submit financials to third parties, for which potential liability can be addressed through a clause limiting use and distribution.

- *Accounting position clauses.* Many times, what the client thinks is acceptable will conflict with professional standards. Establish language stating that accounting positions taken must satisfy professional standards.

- *Supporting documentation.* Remind clients of their responsibility to maintain adequate records to support the accounting records.

Include the proper length of time for which the records should be maintained.

- *Outcome or results.* The engagement letter is a contract, not a marketing device. Do not guarantee outcome or results.

- *Successor and assigns.* To prevent having to ask clients to sign an additional engagement letter if another firm acquires your firm, include successor-and-assigns language.

- *Limitation of liability, consequential damage disclaimers, and limiting the period to commence a lawsuit.* While these clauses are state-specific, their use should not be overlooked.

- *Alternative dispute resolution (ADR).* Coupled with insurance policy benefits (possible reduced deductibles), ADR is one of the lines of defense against malpractice claims.

- *Indemnification and hold-harmless clauses.* Engagement letters does not bind third parties, and many professional liability claims result from third-party suits. Often, the accountant can be reimbursed for losses by implementing indemnification and hold-harmless clauses. A common indemnification is for time spent in providing testimony in tax investigations and inquiries when requested.

- *Review of prior-year accounting records.* State that you are responsible only for positions taken on the current-year records and not for those on previous years' accounting records prepared by another firm.

Sales Cycle Checklist

Keeping track of these steps along the sales cycle process from initial internal exploration to closing and securing a contract can ensure you do not miss anything that could jeopardize your success. Table 5.1 lists all the basic steps that you should follow or at least consider during this simple three-step sales journey. You can change it as needed to fit your particular sales process, but it can offer a good outline or guide to begin with to ensure you don't miss anything through the discovery and qualification, presentation, and engagement letter phases.

Table 5.1 Sales Cycle Checklist

Discovery and Qualification
Contact client with few hours of inquiry
Set up initial meeting
Research the client and vertical industry niche as necessary
Create discovery questions for initial meeting
Conduct in-house discovery exercise prior to meeting
Conduct qualifying review after meeting
Client Presentation
Address client pain points
Determine incentive to start new relationship
Develop service packages
Identify special terms and conditions
Define implementation and support services
Conduct final interval review prior to presentations
Review with client
Conduct negotiations
Engagement Letter
Enlist an attorney to set up letter to reflect your state laws
Begin with one-year agreement
Add 90-day review clause
Outline specific services rendered with fees
Deliver to client for review and approval

HOW AGUILLARD ACCOUNTING CREATED THEIR SUCCESSFUL SALES PROCESS

The following interview was conducted by Amy Vetter with Amanda Aguillard, CPA and Principal of Aguillard Accounting, LLC in New Orleans, Louisiana.

Selling can be difficult—how did you approach the idea of "selling" your services and value as an advisory? What was your main obstacle in terms of selling, and how did you overcome it?

Aguillard: I'm an introvert through and through, although people might be surprised to hear that. I would much rather sit behind a computer and work through spreadsheets than sell to a potential client. What really helped me was to approach lead calls as a chat, not a sales call. I never start a call hoping that the lead will be signed up by the end. I listen to their business and struggles and talk through what possible solutions might look like. However, it's important to keep the implementation details out. This is what they will pay for. Don't drop the candy in the lobby.

What is your sales process? Can you walk through step-by-step what you do, what works, and what happens when something goes wrong that you then need to correct?

Aguillard: Generally our sales process starts with a lead from our website, or a referral. We always set up a 15-minute call—video, if possible—to chat. I only schedule 15 minutes so the client understands that my time is valuable and to keep myself from the temptation of giving too much free advice on this call.

If the client asks to move forward, I'll send an engagement letter right away. I use an automated system that generally requires payment up front. I know that this is unusual for legacy accounting firms, but I have never found it to be a problem. If a client doesn't want to pay now, then he or she probably won't or can't pay later. Accountants need to change the mind-set to position that our time is our product and we can't give it out for free.

Can you offer an example of a sales experiment where you had to change your initial approach and how it helped you to secure a client?

Aguillard: I have had clients who just weren't motivated to commit since we don't force them to. After about the third round of engagement letters and negotiations, I told them that this was the last chance. Of course, I say it nicely but the gist is, "If we are a fit, let's do it; if not, you need to find someone else."

What is the biggest mistake that you see most accountants make when it comes to securing lasting client relationships? What advice would you give in terms of what you have found works for you—and what hasn't—to help a relationship grow and flourish?

Aguillard: Giving away too much free advice. When you do that, the client will never understand the value of what you offer. It's not that we have to be rude or arrogant, but it's really important to set the tone that your knowledge and experience is valuable. A good long-term client will understand.

Thinking back on when you started and learning how to sell—would there have been anything you would have done differently and why?

Aguillard: I would have priced my offerings higher to begin with and would have been more selective in clients I chose to work with. Now we only (1) work with people we like, (2) do work we like, and (3) do work that is profitable. While I say that, I do understand that in the beginning it's not as clear what that means. New practices may not be able to be very selective in what they do, but under no circumstances take work that you hate. It will be miserable and obvious to the client.

CLIENT ONBOARDING PROCESS

Sales are only one-half of the process. The other part is client onboarding. After you have secured the sale, then what? In many ways this is the most crucial aspect of your new client relationship. Now is when clients will look for your guidance as you begin your relationships. If they get frustrated or confused, they will think they made the wrong choice. So you need to make sure the transition from signed engagement letter to beginning services is a smooth one.

Onboarding is the process of getting new clients set up to work with you. The goals of onboarding are to help you both work together effectively, to secure all the information you both need to meet the client's needs and goals, and, perhaps most importantly, to begin your new relationship on the right foot.

Successful onboarding can have far-reaching potential for your cherished advisor business. One benefit is continued service from your client. When you lose a client, all the time and money invested on marketing and developing the relationship has been wasted.

Statistics from the Gartner Group reported online by *Forbes* suggest that 80 percent of a company's future revenue will come from 20 percent of its current customers.[4] However, few businesses devote the necessary marketing resources needed to help retain their current clients, and this becomes a missed opportunity for future revenue and upsell possibilities by retaining your clients.

Another benefit to retaining your current clients is the chance for referrals. When customers are satisfied with the service they receive, they are more likely to share your information with others.

Word-of-mouth can be quite profitable. In fact, an estimated 20 percent to 50 percent of all purchases come from recommendations made by others, according to information from McKinsey & Company.[5]

It takes time, money, and effort to secure new clients, so make sure you have a plan in place to keep them once they sign on. This is where an effective onboarding process comes into play. A smooth onboarding process includes various support tools and platforms, such as face-to-face meetings, video conferences, printed materials, and tasks and reminder schedules. These systems help make your client comfortable during the transition.

Also, keep in mind that creating systems and processes or automating repetitive tasks isn't meant to replace or eliminate your interactions with your clients, but to supplement and enhance them.

Jennifer Bourn of Bourn Creative, who specializes in brand development and content strategy, outlines two parts to a successful new client onboarding campaign:[6]

- *External onboarding process.* What your clients see and experience
- *Internal onboarding process.* What you and your team experience

Here is a look at each one of these processes and how they may operate, according to Bourn.

External

The external onboarding process includes the tasks and actions your client receives and is involved with and is triggered by their initial payment or deposit. A basic external onboarding process for new clients may include items like these:

Welcome
Send a welcome e-mail or a handwritten welcome card by regular mail. Let the client know that he or she will receive additional information in the next few days about the next steps for beginning the relationship.

Kick-Off Call
Schedule an initial 10- to 15-minute project kick-off call to connect personally with your client and communicate key project

information. This will help reaffirm that hiring you was a smart decision and help get your provider/client relationship off to a great start.

Expectations

Discuss exactly what your clients can expect from you—and what you expect of them. Be specific. Also, discuss any major milestones and deadlines.

Process

Review the process your client will go through and communicate major milestones and what's critical to understand at each point.

Education

Provide your client educational and training materials focused on enhancing the project, helping them get clarity and gain focus, and learn the terminology you'll be using throughout the process.

Needs Analysis Questionnaire

Along with performing your own research, it is essential to gather information from your client about the business, site, and objectives. Using a questionnaire the client can complete helps ensure you get all the information you need (see Table 5.2). The answers you receive from the questionnaire(s) will provide a valuable foundation for your future planning and strategy conversations.

Remember, in all of your communications, to constantly remind your clients that you're here to support them and answer any questions they have along the way.

Internal

The internal part of the onboarding process includes all of the support that happens within your team that your clients do not see, although it is integral to the entire accountant–client relationship being as smooth as possible. Just as with the external elements, these internal elements are triggered by the initial receipt of information. Make sure the team has a clear understanding of the client company, its industry, its goals, and the problems it faces. It might be necessary to give your team

Table 5.2 Needs Analysis Questionnaire

Client Name:			
Project Information			
Planned start date:			
Business description:			
Project description:			
Federal ID#:			
Corporate structure			
Fiscal year end: (circle one)	Calendar		Fiscal
Accounting method: (circle one)	Cash	Accrual	Both
Accounting periods: (circle one)	Standard		Custom
General Information			
What accounting system is currently in use?			
How many months of history are to be converted and/or imported?			
Can this data be provided in a CSV format?			
Entity Structure			
How many entities does the company have?			
Does the company have intercompany transactions?			
Revenue and Expense Breakdown			
Does the company use job costing? (Circle one)	Yes		No
Does it have projects? (Circle one)	Yes		No
Does it have locations (Circle one)	Yes		No
Does it have departments? (Circle one)	Yes		No
Cash			
How many bank accounts does the company have?			
Does it use credit cards? (Circle one)	Yes		No
Does it issue any manual checks? (Circle one)	Yes		No
Bank name:			
Account nickname #1:			
Bank routing #:			
Bank account #:			

(continued)

Table 5.2 (*Continued*)

Credit Cards		
Does the company use corporate credit cards? (Circle one)	Yes	No
If so, how many cards?		
Who uses these cards?		
Accounts Payable		
Who will process vendor bills?		
What is the bill approval process?		
Who approves vendor payments?		
What is the company's capitalization policy?		
Employee Payroll & Expenses		
Does the company have payroll?		
How many employees?		
Who is the payroll provider?		
Do company employees submit expenses? If so, how many?		
How often does the company provide reimbursement?		
Revenue and Accounts Receivable		
Does the company invoice customers?		
How many invoices are issued per month?		
Are invoices recurring invoices?		
Does the company have customer contracts?		
Sales Tax		
Does the company charge sales tax?		
If so, in how many states?		
Budgets		
Will the company be using budgets		
Provided by Client		
A complete listing of vendors, including their addresses, phone numbers, contact names, account numbers, 1099 information, payable balances, and recurring expenses.		
Organization-related documents, including articles of incorporation, corporate minutes, and application for federal identification number.		
Copies of bank statements.		

research information and statistics. The more knowledge your team possesses, the better prepared they will be for the initial client interaction. A successful client onboarding process is designed to reduce confusion so clients clearly understand what you need from them. This not only helps the client but your practice, too. The first step to your onboarding process is to look at how your current operation works. What is working well right now? Are there any areas where other clients have struggled? Why is that? Are you repeating tasks? If so, are those tasks necessary, or can you make changes? You get the idea. Use every new onboarding opportunity as a chance to streamline your current processes where possible and make improvements. Eventually, you will design a tried and true process that can be implemented for every new client.

Create an Outline
It needs to highlight the specifics you need from the client. For example:

- What does the client need to know—and why
- What does the client need to learn to help the process?
- What do you need from him or her?
- What does the client need from you—and why
- What are the immediate tasks you need to do?

Once you have clarity about the successes and shortcomings of your current process and what you need to communicate and do, then it's time to get started creating your process. Here are some more strategies from Jennifer Bourn of Bourn Creative:

Outline Each Step
Outline your process from start to finish, creating clear steps, tasks, actions, and key messages

Proof and Test
Remember that your onboarding content is the first exposure your clients will have to your materials, and glaring typos or design mistakes leave a sometimes irreversible bad first impression. Enlist different friends or business owners with varying levels of technical savvy and background to go through the process, reading and

evaluating every component to make sure your information is easy to understand, friendly, and supportive.

Deliver the Content

You can deliver your content in several different ways, such as e-mail, phone, Skype, and Google Hangouts, but remember, not everyone likes these outlets. Many clients like to be able to print and share content with their teams, or read it when they have time.

Ask for Feedback

Let your clients know you welcome their feedback on the materials you provide them. Simply asking shows clients you care about their thoughts and feedback and demonstrates your commitment to quality and constantly improving your level of service.

Be mindful that any system or process you create will no doubt change and evolve as your cherished advisor business grows. You will discover that some aspects work well for every client, while others need to be altered and edited for certain industries or for a client's specific needs.

Evaluating the Process

As you move forward with your onboarding process, take time now and then to evaluate its individual components as well as how it is working overall. A good way to do this is to ask these questions:

- Does the client still have basic questions, or is he/she still confused in any particular area? What can you do to help?
- Is there any part of the process that needs to be tweaked or even changed altogether? Many times you will receive feedback or gain insight into how to make improvements, so don't wait for the next client to implement them. Do it now.
- Are there any parts that could be simplified in any way?

If you identify small changes that need to be made or larger issues that need to be fixed, you must handle them immediately. Otherwise, set aside time annually to review in full every part of your processes and edit or refine it as necessary.

Table 5.3 Onboarding Checklist

External
Send welcome e-mail or handwritten note
Schedule kick-off call
Share expectations and review major milestones and deadlines
Review process client will go through
Provide necessary education and training materials
Provide questionnaire for additional client/business information
Internal
Complete needs analysis with client
Create project plan
Brief team on client's industry, goals, and specific problems
Set up CRM system to automate internal processes
Check in with client to review status after 30 days
Review Current Onboarding Process
Outline entire process for clear steps, actions, and key messages
Review/change content as needed
Proof and text content with friends and business owners
Reviewing delivery methods of the content
Ask for feedback from clients

Onboarding Checklist

It takes time to perfect your onboarding process, and no doubt you will have a learning curve at first. As you move forward, you will learn what works and what doesn't until eventually you will create a process that works for both you and your client. The onboarding checklist in Table 5.3 summarizes the main steps of the onboarding process to ensure you stay on track and meet all your objectives.

CREATING A PROJECT PLAN

After you have met with your client and gathered all the necessary information during the onboarding and engagement letter process, you need to outline your services in a project plan. This document outlines how both you and the client can track the agreed-upon services and provides a breakdown of costs and time allocated for each task.

A project plan helps both parties. For the client, the plan shows exactly what services you will provide so the client can get a better understanding of your value and how much time you devote to the project.

For the accountant, the project plan has several upsides. It's another tool that helps strengthen the communication between your team and the client. It also helps to document how much time is being spent for each task—and who performs them—which helps you stay on budget.

Too often, we end up doing more than agreed upon in order to just get the work completed and to keep the client happy. But this approach cuts into your budget and ultimately your profits. It's important you don't give away your time for free, or else you will set that expectation for the future. If circumstances arise in which a designated task takes longer to complete, or if the client asks for something else within a certain task that requires extra time, you should bill for that. The project plan helps to proactively let the client know that a task may go over budget because of out-of-scope reasons and allows you to communicate that in real time before you complete the work. This approach helps facilitate a better relationship with your client; the client can decide whether they want to spend more or not, rather than getting a surprise bill from your firm for overages that you didn't communicate prior to performing the work.

For example, if you did a kitchen renovation, the contractor's bid would include all the work that you agreed to within a designated time frame. However, if the contractor is in the middle of one task—for instance, installing the floor—and you want him or her to change the material or add extra sealant, you will be charged extra for that, and they will issue a change order for the difference in the original scope.

This is no different than how you and your client will work, and the project plan protects you from doing more than what was agreed to without extra compensation.

Finally, the project plan helps you monitor your team's work schedule and time. You can see who is working on each task and which team members are involved. This can help you arrange your team's individual responsibilities to better match their skills. For instance, for quick-turnaround task, some members might be more qualified than others, while certain members are better at longer, more detail-oriented assignments.

Once your project plan is created, you can upload it to your customer relationship management (CRM) system (as discussed in the next section) or other project management software for your entire team to see in real time and note any changes or updates. You can also add extra details and notes to this version that your internal team needs to see, but not necessarily your client. For the client, send updated plans as tasks are completed.

How detailed your project plan is depends on the client and the scope of services and tasks. Table 5.4 is a short sample of what a project plan might entail—you can use this as a foundation for building your plan.

Table 5.4 Project Plan

	Total Project Budget		**190.50**
I	**Project Management**		**45.50**
	1	Hand off from pre-sales	0.50
	2	Kick-off meeting	2.00
	3	Finalize work plan and schedule	1.00
	4	Report project status/attend status meetings	42.00
II	**Requirements—Needs Analysis**		**27.00**
	1	Gather and review required reports	1.50
		Review chart of accounts	1.00
		Review items	0.50
	2	Review business process	3.50
		General ledger	2.00
		Accounts payable	0.50
		Accounts receivable	0.50
		Cash management	0.50
	3	Review and document needs analysis	22.00

(continued)

Table 5.4 (*Continued*)

III	**Configuration**		**26.00**
	1	Company	2.25
		Provision organization	1.00
		Create users	1.00
		User permissions	0.25
	2	General ledger	2.25
		Create or import chart of accounts	2.25
	3	Accounts payable (A/P)	2.50
		Create A/P terms	0.25
		Create or import vendors	2.25
	4	Accounts receivable (A/R)	2.25
		Create A/R terms	0.25
		Create or import customers	2.00
	5	Cash management	2.50
		Create bank/credit card accounts	2.50
IV	**System Integration**		**17.00**
		Selection of add-on systems	5.00
		Map add-ons to application programming interface (API)	10.00
		Test for accuracy	2.00
V	**Report Development**		**12.00**
	1	Customize vertical industry report templates	8.00
	2	Create management financial reporting packages	4.00
VI	**Data Migration**		**36.00**
		Beginning balances	20.00
		Historical monthly activity—2 years	4.00
		Open A/R invoices	8.00
		Open A/P bills	4.00
VII	**Develop User Procedures & Training**		**19.00**
		General ledger	2.00
		Purchasing	2.00
		Sales	3.00
		Cash management and budgeting	2.00
		Employee expenses	3.00
		Payroll processing	7.00
VIII	**Training**		**8.00**
		Training	8.00

HOW APTUS ACCOUNTING & ADVISORY DEVELOPED ITS SALES PROCESS AND CLIENT RELATIONSHIPS

The following interview was conducted by Amy Vetter with James Solomons, CA, Partner, and Co-Founder of Aptus Accounting & Advisory in Baulkham Hills, Australia.

What has been your biggest obstacle when it comes to client interaction and impression (making that initial connection with potential clients) with a vertical niche team?

Solomons: The biggest challenge we have faced when entering new markets is you get a lot of "tire kickers" as well as potential clients who have no idea about the value we create and the fees we charge. To give the right impression, we always try to keep our messaging consistent and have a good online presence. Our aim is for potential clients that have come from a nonreferral source to have an idea of who we are and what we do before they contact us. We always tell our story and share our WHY. We try to qualify all leads from nonreferral sources via a phone call first, too. This allows us to understand their need for our services and to determine if they are a right fit. We don't discuss fees. If they demand it, we let them go and don't move to stage two. If they pass this phase then we meet with them.

What did you find was the greatest challenge with initial client interaction? What did you learn and what did you do to overcome?

Solomons: Our firm is tech based and moving to fixed monthly fees, and many new clients are new to this. They are used to time-based billing along with paper and pen accounting. So we needed to educate our clients as they come onboard, and even in initial sessions, about why we work this way, but more importantly how it benefits them. Many accountants forget or decline to tell this to their new or potential clients. We take this opportunity to begin selling our value to them and explain how working with us will help them grow their business by supporting them in real time—not just meeting them a few times a year. When a client hears this, for them it's a no-brainer. Once we have this buy-in, the rest of the relationship is easy to manage.

How did you create your marketing strategy? What did you decide to focus on and what was your strategy for implementing?

Solomons: Our marketing strategy began with "how did we want to be viewed" in each respective area we wanted to market. We looked at peers in the area and what they were doing. For instance, we studied the audience and the type of content already being delivered. We asked the question, "Do we want to be different or do we want to deliver information in a way that is already being delivered, but be better at it?" Once we decided on our language and approach, we then set about building a marketing calendar for this area to deliver content at the right time in the year.

Our main focus is always on content marketing. It's always about education and showing readers/viewers our capabilities to deliver solutions, not just talk the talk. One area we have always been good at is the tech space and our approach is to develop blogs and content around the cloud and how technology can benefit SMBs [small and mid-sized businesses]. We created a calendar around this to ensure we were pushing our message at peak switch times. Blogs, newsletters, and associated social posts are all part of the campaign.

What was your greatest marketing challenge, and how did you overcome it?

Solomons: The greatest challenge is remaining consistent. The occasional blog post from a content marketing perspective is not going to win us clients. Consistent posts, covering a range of topics in our niche area, help to build a following and level of trust with our current and potential clients. They begin to expect each new post.

When we developed our marketing strategy, we looked at the themes we wanted to cover and then set aside adequate time to develop the content—from brainstorming to crafting to reviewing—to ensure we had perfected the message. If we had a campaign that lasted three weeks and required 10 separate types of content (tweets, blogs, etc.) we would set aside time one to two months beforehand to complete. And not just 30 minutes here or there, but full two- to three-hour time blocks.

Selling can be difficult—how did you approach the idea of "selling" your services and value as an advisory? What was your main obstacle in terms of selling and how did you overcome it?

Solomons: The hardest part is getting that buy-in from the clients, and sometimes it takes time. We never hard sell, and a client will come to us when they are ready, especially when it comes to advisory services. When a client pushes back, we often offer some free work to help secure the deal.

What is your sales process? Can you walk through step-by-step what you do, what works, and what happens when something goes wrong that you then need to correct?

Regardless of how the lead comes in, it goes into our sales pipeline. This generates our lead template. It works like this:

- The first part is always a phone call to qualify the lead. Are they a right fit?
- Second is a scoping session with the potential client to see if they pass the qualifying stage. Here is when we find out their needs.
- Next, we put together a proposal. Turnaround is always 24 hours or less.
- We then present the proposal and talk through the solutions. We always tie it back to the problems they need solved and the value we are creating. The figures are always clear and transparent.
- If the client agrees, we move them to the secured phase and our client implementation team takes over and begins the onboarding.
- If we get the proposal wrong, or the fee seems too high for the client, we simply say, "It looks like we have got your needs wrong. What do we need to adjust?" We never discount. We remove services from the proposal to bring the cost down or change the scope.

Can you offer an example of a sales experiment where you had to change your initial approach and how it helped you to secure a client?

Solomons: When we first started rolling out Futrli (Crunchboards), we made a decision to give it to every client for free. The aim was that they would love the free boards and then engage us to do more work. We created some simple boards for each client and then invited them via an e-mail introduction. Yet it was not as successful as we hoped. Few clients logged in and even fewer called us about it.

So we began from scratch and decided to send each client a PDF printout of their board—showing them what they could now see—and then a week later followed up with a call to discuss their views and about getting them access. Just by placing this call to explain what it was all about (even though it was the same script as the e-mail) made a huge difference. The clients now understood it and were keen to try. This resulted in more clients engaging us to do more advisory work.

What is the biggest mistake that you see most accountants make when it comes to securing lasting client relationships? What advice would you give in terms of what you have found works for you—and what hasn't—to help a relationship grow and flourish?

Solomons: A client relationship is like any other relationship. It requires effort to maintain. I think many accountants take longer relationships for granted and expect that because they have won it, the client will be a client for life. These days it is really easy to switch accountants, due in part to technology and the cloud.

What doesn't work for us is expecting that technology can replace the human side of the relationship. Our clients love the streamlined way we do business with them, but still want to have a conversation with us, even if it's via Skype.

What does work is constantly looking for ways to add more value, at little or no cost to the client. Clients constantly challenge the value we provide, so we are always trying to keep them happy. It's not that they don't value us, but they always want more out of their investment.

The other way is to treat our clients like equals and as smart business owners. We are no better than them, nor are they any better than us. It's a business relationship where each party derives value, and so when things are not going well, we have honest conversations with them. They respect that.

A great example of this is when we have had start-up businesses quickly grow. We offer packages to start-ups in their first one to two years that are designed to ease a start-up cash flow burden. Sometimes they grow fast, but we still charge them the "start-up rates," even though they need us more and more. We have suffered in the past when we have continued to do the extra work, essentially for free, and as a result the standard of work declines, and in some case, the client has left citing our level of service as being less than promised. To combat this, we simply have a discussion with the start-up and explain how their demands have increased and that to support them properly, our fees need to go up, too. They grumble, but it's not personal. They just want to save every dollar, but they often agree and the relationship stays strong.

Thinking back on when you started and learned how to sell, would there have been anything you would have done differently?

Solomons: Looking back, the biggest mistake (and this is industry-wide really) is to undercharge just to get the client in the door. This sets some relationships up to fail, as it creates a huge expectation from the client that fees were cheap, and it essentially undervalues what we do. It is so hard to move these clients onto higher fees, or at least fees that equal the service being delivered. We have found we have to charge appropriately from day one for each service delivered.

Is there any other advice or anything else you want to share in the areas of client impressions, sales, and marketing that you would offer other accountants with their clients (or potential clients)?

Solomons: Always look at the services you deliver from the client's perspective. Would you buy your own service? Is the new technology you have implemented making it easier for clients to deal with you, or is this just making it easier for you and now the client has three portals to log into for different things? The client pays the fees, so if they are not able to deal with you easily, they will go elsewhere.

AUTOMATING YOUR INTERNAL PROCESSES WITH CRM

Customer relationship management (CRM) is a technology system that is used to track leads and current client opportunities, such as when proposals have been sent out and signed. A CRM system tracks client campaigns and shows whether they are successful. There are many CRM software applications available. A good way to find examples of CRM systems that are used by other accounting and bookkeeping practices is by doing searches on marketplace sites for your cloud accounting provider. A CRM can help identify the most profitable clients in terms of highest profit margins and most revenue. You can use this information to consider providing your top clients a different level of services. A CRM also can help you identify high-value customers for possible upsell or referral opportunities.

Here are five specific designs to look for, according to Inc.com:[7]

■ *Application programming interface (API).* This interface allows the CRM to link with other systems so that you don't need to enter information multiple times. You especially want to ensure that it integrates with your cloud accounting application so you can enter client information once and allow it to be shared between the systems.

- *Multiple contact information*. This feature allows you to organize and access information by a person's name and company.
- *Dashboards*. This offers a summary of the sales opportunities underway across your customer base and which team members is working on them.
- *Delegation*. Your team should be able to electronically delegate tasks to members, especially through the client onboarding process or ongoing support of a client.
- *Information entry and access*. You should be able to enter and access information from anywhere within the system.

Project List

Maintain a project list that highlights all your clients, ongoing projects, and deadlines, as well as the current status of each task related to the projects, to ensure you are on pace to meet all deadlines. You also can automate this through your CRM.

Check-In

You should check in with your clients 30 days after implementing a new system. This is a chance to get valuable feedback from your client, address any concerns, and get an overall feeling of how everything is going. Prepare a list of questions prior to the meeting as well as a list of all the work you have accomplished so far. Remember, the client may not "see" your services, and thus your value, so it is a good idea to remind him or her when necessary.

Implementing the proper systems and processes is one of the best investments you can make to ensure you retain clients. Communication is key. There is no such thing as overcommunicating. It is critical to the client feeling comfortable and not getting lost in the process. These systems you put in place not only empower you to delegate and automate, but it will give you greater confidence in your service quality and you'll enjoy less stress knowing that things are being taken care of and not slipping through the cracks.

SUMMARY

Traditionally, accountants, by nature, are not in the business of selling their services, but instead have had clients come to them from their geographic area. But in this new technology age, potential clients are outside of your 10-mile radius, so learning how to sell your services becomes increasingly important. You not only need to make connections with potential clients through your marketing efforts, social media engagement, and industry networking, but when you do make that connection, you need to show why you are valuable to a client through all the wonderful services you offer that can help to improve his or her life. A simple three-step sales process—discovery and qualification, client presentation, and engagement letter—can help identify potential clients and then help guide you through the procedure in which you present your services and fees and then arrange and secure contracts. Once you have established a new relationship with a client, the onboarding phase helps bring the client into the relationship through training, support, and constant engagement to build a long-lasting relationship.

ENDNOTES

1. Shelley F. Hall, "10 Reasons Why Discovery Questioning is the Key to Closing Business," May 2017, Precision Market Group, https://www.precisionmarketinggroup.com/blog/bid/80507/10-Reasons-Why-Discovery-Questioning-is-the-Key-to-Closing-Business.
2. Phyllis Weiss Haserot, *The Marketer's Handbook of Tips & Checklists* (New York: West, 2010).
   Phyllis Weiss Haserot helps organizations solve inter-generational challenges among work colleagues and with clients to achieve better productivity and knowledge transfer, retention, succession planning, and business development results. Phyllis is president of Practice Development Counsel, business development consulting and coaching, and author of *The Rainmaking Machine* (Thomson Reuters, 2017) and *The Marketer's Handbook of Tips & Checklists* (West/Thomson Reuters, 2011).
   Email: pwhaserot@pdcounsel.com
   Website: www.pdcounsel.com
   LinkedIn: www.linkedin.com/in/pwhaserot
   Twitter: @phylliswhaserot
3. John F. Raspante, CPA, and Stephen Vono, "Engagement Letters for the Individual Tax Practitioner," January 1, 2014, *Journal of Accountancy*, http://www.journalofaccountancy.com/issues/2014/jan/20137591.html.

4. Alex Lawrence, "Five Customer Retention Tips for Entrepreneurs," November 1, 2012, *Forbes*, https://www.forbes.com/sites/alexlawrence/2012/11/01/five-customer-retention-tips-for-entrepreneurs/#18626e795e8d.

5. Jacques Bughin, Jonathan Doogan, and Ole Jørgen Vetvik, "A New Way to Measure Word-of-Mouth Marketing," April 2010, *McKinsey Quarterly*, http://www.mckinsey.com/business-functions/marketing-and-sales/our-insights/a-new-way-to-measure-word-of-mouth-marketing.

6. Jennifer Bourn, "How to Implement a New Client Onboarding Process and Set Expectations," January 19, 2015, Bourn Creative, http://www.bourncreative.com/implement-new-client-onboarding-process-set-expectations/.

7. "How to Use Customer Relationship Management Software," n.d., *Inc.com*, https://www.inc.com/guides/cust_relation/20909.html.

CHAPTER 6

Building Lasting Relationships

The best client is the one who lasts and continues wanting your services. Securing long-term client–accountant relationships is the ultimate goal to help to build and grow your cherished advisor business. As I discussed at the beginning of this book with the story of my grandfather, an accountant can become a strategic consultant and an integral part of your clients' business future.

When you have established yourself as a cherished advisor with a client, the additional rewards you can reap from the relationship can appear in different ways. When you have shown your clients how you can help them—and in return they begin to see the results in their businesses—they are more inclined to reach out to you for other services.

For instance, if you begin your relationship with a basic-level package of services, and you are delivering value and a better experience than the client expected, your client may want additional service offerings from your practice. As you have learned in previous chapters, when you deliver advisory services, you become more invested in how a client's business operates as you become more acquainted with their short- and long-term goals. This in turn opens up discussions for a client to ask for advice in other matters because you are their central point of contact for advice and referrals. For example, the client could ask for advice in areas that you don't offer, such as asking about potential realtors you may know because the client is looking to move to a larger facility, or asking your advice about new equipment purchases—not only how the purchases might affect their tax write offs, but also how they may affect the business now and in the future. The more a client values your relationship, the more he or she will want the partnership to grow stronger and flourish. Plus, when clients value your services, they are more likely to recommend you to others, which is the best and most cost-effective way to get new business.

This is the kind of trusted relationship you want to develop. However, as with any type of relationship, it takes work and commitment to make it last. If you put the relationship on autopilot and expect everything to be good, you are setting you and your business up for eventual failure. Additionally, to continually create value, it's important for you to continue to make contacts and network with other experts, so that whenever a client has a need, you have someone to whom you can refer them. The ultimate goal is for you to be a central point of contact for your clients so that you hear about the things they want to do in their businesses first and can ensure they are working with people you trust as advisors and experts as well.

Your client relationship is not just about numbers and figures. There is a saying: "People may forget what you say, but they never forget how you make them feel." People remember experiences more than that just the offer of a product or service, and it is this experience that keeps them coming back. Look at Apple. Their focus is not on the wonderful things the latest iPad or iPhone can do, but about the experience of buying and using it. That is why they put such emphasis on making their Apple stores so appealing and stimulating, and why they offer personal on-site support and invest in elegant packaging. It is about making the customer feel special and important. That is what they are selling and that is why people keep coming back. The experience you create in your firm with your clients can follow the example of Apple—emphasizing the experience of how you deliver your services.

When most businesses launch a start-up, they tend to focus too much on the product and then try to fold in customer experience later. In his book, *X: The Experience When Business Meets Design*, Brian Solis, a prominent thought leader in business innovation, makes the point that good customer experience tends to happen by accident and not design, and that needs to change.[1] The advantage you have as a cherished advisor is that you can design this experience with your client, providing access to great technology, a specialized team, and a great onboarding experience that can help put the client at the forefront of your services.

For instance, the virtual availability you create can be a powerful customer experience you can offer—for both your team and your client. As I previously discussed, attracting new talent like millennials means offering them innovative ways to work and interact. Setting up virtual offices and video interaction is appealing to this generation, as it brings down the walls of traditional office settings and creates a collaborative culture where everybody works together as a team. Your millennial staff isn't the only group who wants this—so do your clients.

This dynamic experience is something that your clients will appreciate, as they will not just work with a single individual, but rather a robust, multipurpose team attending to their needs, answering their questions, and helping to grow their businesses proactively.

One of the main keys to building lasting relationships is to keep the line of communication open and to interact on a regular basis, but it also involves receiving feedback from the client, too. Just because a client renews their contract with you does not mean that he or she is necessarily happy with the relationship. The client simply may be too busy to look for another accountant. You are "okay" in his or her mind, so the client will rely on you to perform your basic services, but that is as far as the relationship will go. Alternatively, it just may be too much work to look for another accountant to replace you. To become a cherished advisor, you need your relationship to become more personal and connected, rather than providing the same experience they could get from anyone else.

The process begins the moment you secure a contract with your client. You want to establish certain protocols that send a clear message to your client that he or she is important and you are invested in him/her. Here is a checklist of everyday actions and protocol you and your team need to ensure you always follow at the beginning of any client relationship. Many of these suggestions are simple business courtesies, but they lay the foundation for what you hope the relationship becomes, and they keep the client happy. Some of these will be assigned to individuals on your team, while others are steps that the entire team can embrace.

Return the Customer's Phone Calls Promptly

Have you ever had to wait for someone to get back with you? How did it make you feel? By returning calls quickly, you tell your clients that they are a priority. You can set up an operations team that is responsible for returning these calls, as I discussed in the staffing model section of Chapter 3.

Reply to E-mails at Predictable Intervals During the Day

While you don't necessarily have to respond to every e-mail as soon as possible, create scheduled times during the day (morning, afternoon, and before the work day ends) to respond to all inquiries. If you set up a customer relationship management (CRM) system for your office (discussed later in the previous chapter), your clients' e-mail requests can be tracked there and assigned out to the appropriate team members by your operations team.

Create an Internal Help Desk for Clients

The purpose of having a help desk team to support your employees and clients is so your revenue-generating staff can stay focused on their work rather than getting side-tracked by one-off requests. As discussed before, you can use an internal support ticketing system through your CRM to manage these client requests. Having the help desk team offers clients the added security of knowing there is an entire internal team available to them when issues arise.

Build a Library of E-mail Templates that Address Typical Questions

This way you don't have to create them from scratch each time. Share these draft e-mails across your teams. This way, when someone asks a question, your team can e-mail back the response quickly and only tailor the necessary parts. This is a big timesaver for your practice, and it keeps clients happy because they are getting a quick response.

Add Graphs to Their Financial Reports from Your Financial Analysis

It is a simple act, and it does not add more to your workload, but it has two main outcomes: (1) it helps the client visualize the financial information and thus better understand what it means, and (2) it shows an extra effort to satisfy for the client. It can also be an upsell opportunity if the client wants that kind of information on a more routine basis.

Keep Track of Important Business Events in a Client's Professional Life

For example, when is the client's worker's comp up for renewal? You can possibly bring in an expert (if you aren't one) to help them save money. You can also create automatic responders within the software you use to alert your clients of sales tax or payroll tax deadlines, if you are not handling that for them. Those little extras can go a long way with your clients' happiness with your service.

Ask Your Client What They Expect from You

Note the answers in the client's file, and make sure you live up to them.

Stay Up-to-Date on Simple Market Research in the Client's Industry

Share the information with him or her on a regular basis or during your scheduled appointments. Another option is to convene a client advisory panel: Invite clients to lunch to discuss new services you are offering, or bring in experts in their industries that they can ask questions to. You can in turn use this information to improve your services, and use it as content for your next business newsletter.

Keep Up-to-Date on Industry News

This way, you can discuss trends with your clients as well as share information. Your clients may not always have the time to be up-to-date on industry information, and they can learn to entrust you to provide valued insight.

CREATING PERSONALIZED VIRTUAL RELATIONSHIPS

Personal engagement does not always have to be on site and in person, and after you have established an initial connection with your new client, virtual meetings and communication is often preferred, especially if you have clients in other geographic areas that are not in driving distance.

The technology of virtual interaction that has helped you recruit a new generation of talent can be used to better enhance your client interactions—with you and/or other members of your team. There are many advantages to this. For instance, it creates a time-saving mechanism through which you can engage your client without the need for travel. Also, the flexibility of virtual interaction means you can communicate at all hours of the day, which helps your client as it's not seen as a distraction from the course of regular business. It also allows you to share information and files in real time so you can review and discuss information together or alert the client to a situation that requires immediate attention. Creating this type of setup can further help with training the client on new software platforms or reviewing priority items in real time. Further, virtual interaction enables you to greatly expand your pool of potential clients. At first, you no doubt will be focused on nearby vertical industry niche clients, but as you grow and expand, you can market to clients across the country and even around the world.

The best type of virtual engagement depends on your clients and what they are most comfortable with. You should offer a few different ways for them to communicate with you. Sometimes, a client might already be familiar with one type of technology, in which case it's best to stick with that, but often the client may defer to your judgment in terms of selecting the best technology for the engagement. There are a lot of video conferencing and file sharing program out there, but here is a look at some popular technology applications that you can use:

Cisco WebEx (webex.com)

WebEx allows you to record your meetings and include multiple feed or side-by-side with screen-sharing viewing.

Dropbox (dropbox.com)

Have a lot of information that you need to share with others? Dropbox can hold all types and sizes of files—from documents to photos to audio files—and allow you to share them with people. Plus you can access it from anywhere from synched devices or even through Dropbox's website.

Google Drive (google.com/drive)

Like Dropbox, Google Drive allows you to file and share documents and can be shared with team members who can access it anytime. Another feature of Google Drive is Google Docs where people can write and edit on the same document and add comments and instant chats.

GoToMeeting/GoToWebinar (gotomeeting.com)

The advantages of this service include live 24/7 support and unlimited monthly meetings.

Join Me (join.me)

This program allows up to 10 individuals to view your screen at the same time. It's ideal for big group meetings like brainstorming sessions and presentations.

Skype (skype.com)

The video conferencing app works on smartphones, tablets, and computers, and is ideal when you need to host large video calls as it can accommodate up to 25 people. The program also offers language translation.

Slack (slack.com)

Meetings can be organized into open or private channels. Bonus: people can add comments or messages to the conversation.

Zoom (zoom.us)

What is great about Zoom is that you can share up to 50 HD video streams at once. You can also do video, audio, screen sharing, and group messaging.

CREATING TOUCH POINTS TO STAY ENGAGED

To ensure you maintain a strong connection with your client you have to create multiple "touch points," which are ways to stay engaged with your client. Not just courtesy check-ins, these touch points are communication with a purpose. This way, the client will always see value in your communication efforts and not just something you do as an empty gesture.

At first, these touch points may be scheduled biweekly or weekly as you go over initial set-up and procedures and check whether the client has any questions or concerns. Eventually, these meetings may be reserved for weekly, bimonthly, or monthly get-togethers as both parties become more comfortable working together. You don't want to have the meetings too far apart, as the client may start to feel that he/she is not a priority, which can risk the future potential of your relationship.

These get-togethers can be face-to-face, phone calls, or virtual conferencing, or some combination of the three. In-person is best at first, as it helps build a personal connection, but if the client's schedule does not allow it or he/she is uncomfortable with face-to-face, suggest the other methods.

When you arrange these meetings, always make sure they are constructive. Your clients' time is valuable, and they will not want to see these meetings as a waste of their time. If you bring something of value to your clients, they will be much more willing to embrace the meetings and see their real value. You can learn a lot about how to interact with potential clients through trial and error. Here are some guidelines to follow:

Prepare an Agenda

Ask the client beforehand if there is anything in particular he or she wants to cover. Write up an agenda that includes the client's items and yours, and send it to the client at least a week before you meet so they have time to review. Knowing what the meeting will entail helps the client gather any information they need to make the meeting more productive.

Do the Necessary Research

Research the main issues and any questions the client has so you can address them during your meeting. This way, you will not get stuck not knowing something. If the client asks a question you aren't prepared for, that is okay. Let him or her know you will research it following the meeting and get back with a response soon.

Look Professional and Act Professionally

Professional appearance and mannerisms are, of course, essential at the beginning of the client relationship. You want to reflect an image of knowledge and confidence so the client feels comfortable. However, as the client relationship progresses, there may be a tendency to relax that attention to detail. Don't. Approach every meeting like it's the first one.

Set Client Office Meetings

Visit the client's workplace whenever possible. It not only saves the client travel time, but he or she is in a comfortable and relaxed environment, and you can meet others in the company to make more personal connections as well. If you do host a meeting at your office, set up in a conference room or other place away from the day-to-day hustle of office noise and chatter.

Begin and End Every Meeting on Time

Arrive early and be ready to begin the meeting on time. Again, this shows your professionalism by showing how much you value the client's time. At the end, announce when there are only about five to 10 minutes left to finish up, in case you need to address something on the agenda that hasn't been covered. When you finish, go ahead and schedule the next meeting right when you are with them. It's much harder to get your next appointment after a meeting through e-mail and phone calls. This ensures you can coordinate a time while you are still together.

Keep the Meeting on Track

Bring a copy of the agenda in case the client doesn't have it. Summarize what you both will go over and then address each point. Also, ask the client before you begin whether he or she wants to change the agenda or move up a topic to discuss first if there is something new and more pressing he/she needs to talk about.

Send a Summary of the Meeting

When you return to your office, prepare and e-mail a summary of what was discussed, any decisions that were made, and any additional information or services the client has requested. This ensures nothing was missed during the meeting and creates backup documentation in case either you or the client needs to revisit the decisions you documented.

HOW FARNELL CLARKE LIMITED BUILT AND MAINTAINED THEIR CLIENT AND TEAM RELATIONSHIPS

The following interview was conducted by Amy Vetter with Will Farnell, FCCA, Director of Farnell Clarke Limited, Norfolk, United Kingdom.

What is your approach to maintaining lasting client relationships? Can you share examples of what you do to keep long-standing clients, as well as an example of when you were at risk for losing a client—what did you do to reaffirm the relationship and why did it work?

Farnell: We view every touch point we have with a client as an opportunity to build on a relationship rather than an opportunity to charge our time. In the early days, we were unique in offering true fixed-fee services, and I would use the analogy of a client popping in to chat over a coffee. Many firms would see this as billable advisory time, but for me it was a chance to get to know our clients better, understand the challenges they were facing, and most importantly look at ways we could add more value to our relationship. It is about looking at the lifetime value of a client, rather than "have we recovered the right level of fees this year?"

What are the greatest obstacles you have encountered for building lasting client relationships, and why? What did you do to overcome?

Farnell: The greatest challenges are when we take on clients that are not the right kind, as their expectations are not aligned with ours. Over time, we have realized that clients have to fit our style for us to create long-lasting, valuable relationships. We have therefore become more conscious of assessing the fit with all prospective clients and are not being afraid to suggest we may not be the right firm for them.

What have you learned from a client relationship that eventually fell away that you have applied for ongoing relationships?

Farnell: As a firm, we have seen growth at 40 percent year on year for the last 10 years. This means the dynamic of some of the older client relationships has changed. In some cases this has led to clients moving on, as we did not put in place continuity as the pressure on the firm's principals increased. We now ensure that staffs at different levels are involved in the client relationship to help reduce the risk of relationships being neglected as the business grows or staff moves on.

Building relationships with your teams is equally important. What special or differentiated compensation programs, benefits, or rewards do you put in place to differentiate your workplace and keep employees happy? How do they work and why have they been successful?

Farnell: We are a firm of 32 staff and fall into the difficult space of being too big to be small—and too small to be big. We can't offer the same pay levels as our larger regional competitors. We recognize that the millennial generation will account for 75 percent of the workplace by 2025. Our own workforce is already at this level for this demographic. We therefore invested heavily last year in a new office fit out. We introduced a number of break-out work areas, provided MacBooks to allow staff to work flexibly, created a fun and engaging workplace, and even included a pub-themed meeting room complete with bar and pool table.

Identifying great talent is challenging—are there any special interview techniques you have put in place that have been successful in identifying the right candidates for your practice?

Farnell: We have always been laid back around interviews. We want candidates to get a feel for the culture and ethos of our business. The last interview we did was on a Friday afternoon, so the candidate became involved in Friday afternoon social time involving beer in our office pub. The interview finished with a game of pool. I'm not saying this is the answer, but we got a great sense that the candidate would be a good cultural fit with the firm.

How have you identified successors for leadership roles in your practice? Do you let them know? Do you have mentorship programs? What skills do you look for in potential leaders to mentor?

Farnell: I have informally mentored a number of staff over the last 10 years. One team member has since taken up a director's role. We are now more conscientious to identify talent early on, and we work to support the staff to ensure they get the right opportunities to foster and develop skills that are valuable to us as a business.

INTERPERSONAL AWARENESS TO SUCCEED AS AN ADVISOR: COLLABORATION, INFLUENCE, NEGOTIATION, AND COMMUNICATION

Your personal skills are also a key part of establishing long-standing client relationships. This is often an area where many professionals might struggle. Many of us go into the field we do because of the technical expertise we want to gain, but the personal interaction and skills to be successful are not as much of a focus.

Personal skills are often referred to as "soft" skills and include areas like overall communication, collaboration (teamwork), influence (critical thinking and analyzing situations), and negotiation (problem solving). Soft skills can also include areas related to leadership and project management.

How important are soft skills? *The Capability Gap 2015*, a report from Hays plc, a global specialist recruitment firm, asked what skills are most important to an organization's future success. The survey found that almost the same percentages of employers and of accountancy and finance employees valued soft skills as almost equal to acquired skills like understanding IT and software systems, commercial awareness, and industry knowledge.

Specifically, 57 percent of employers and 55 percent of employees rated communication as the top soft skill needed, followed by leadership (44 percent and 40 percent respectively) and collaboration and team working (44 percent and 47 percent respectively).[2]

These skills are valuable for your team to improve competency—a team member's ability to analyze a client's problems and provide insight into strategies to help improve the situation and thus the client's business is critical to being successful as an advisor. From the client's perspective, these skills help influence the client to make decisions one way or another and provide a level of experience to give the client comfort that he or she is getting significant value from the investment.

Even if team members lack certain natural abilities, they can still be taught. Begin by meeting with each member and sharing which soft skills they think they excel at and where they feel they need to improve. These one-on-one interactions help team members open up and have an honest discussion about their needs and shortfalls, which provides an opportunity to identify training needs beyond the technical skills. Additionally, creating teams where different strengths and weaknesses offset each other can provide a level of success as a group that might not happen individually.

But perhaps the most vital step is to lead by example. Your workplace environment offers a platform to encourage the team to develop these skills—beginning with you. Show your team why these soft skills are so important for them, the team, and the business—and how lacking certain skills is not a form of weakness, but rather an opportunity for improvement and growth.

Begin with yourself and highlight what soft skills you lack and what you plan to do to improve. An important initiative that can enhance your team's soft skills is to expose them to professional training. For example, you could host sales seminars, voice instruction, or team-building conferences.

Another method is to begin a mentoring program. Most successful teams are made up of members who have skillsets that complement one another, so use that to your advantage. Pair up team members so they can learn more about each other's strengths.

Do you have someone who is more reserved? Have that person work with a teammate that is a more accomplished speaker, who can accompany the reserved person to client meetings or presentations. Also, take advantage of opportunities for members to improve their skills during regular business activities. For instance, you can have a team member lead a training session internally or externally to present a client strategy.

You can also motivate team members by tying soft-skill improvement into individual and team goals and linking it to bonus opportunities. For instance, an entire team or individual team members can receive bonuses if they attend self-improvement classes or team-building seminars that result in securing a client renewal or resolving specific concerns a client may have.

Measure Client Satisfaction with a Net Promoter Score

As your client relationship matures and you both have established a solid working rhythm, it is a good idea to measure the client's satisfaction with your services. As mentioned earlier, renewing your services does not mean the client is happy or the relationship is a success. Happy, loyal clients are the best way to grow your cherished advisor business. Loyalty is a client's willingness to recommend your services to someone else—another business colleague, a friend, or a family member. When a client does this, he or she is in essence making an investment in you and is willing to put his or her reputation on the line.

Recommendations are not always easy to measure since you don't know when (or if) a client will show this type of loyalty. For this reason, it's crucial to check in and measure how much the client values your services and where you could improve. This type of measurement of client satisfaction is much more valuable to you than a renewed contract with no reason attached to it.

One of the best and most-often used tools to help gauge your client loyalty is the Net Promoter Score (NPS). This is an alternative to usual customer satisfaction research and is quite popular with many top companies. In fact, according to statistics from *Bloomberg.com*, more than two-thirds of Fortune 1000 companies use this metric.[3]

The NPS is a rating system that ranges from minus 100 to plus 100. It measures how willing customers may be to recommend your products or services. An NPS score is also used to help gauge your client's overall satisfaction with your services.

People don't like to fill out in-depth customer satisfaction surveys, which is why they can't be used as valuable information. Not enough people fill them out, and/or they do not offer the insight a company needs. The NPS is superior: It's easy to understand and quick to complete, as it only involves three questions and grading on a 1-to-10 scale.

The NPS also can be used as a motivational method for your team to help improve client satisfaction, as low scores tend to indicate poor client satisfaction. They can work to improve the NPS and, by doing so, correct problems your client may experience before the situation becomes worse.

How the NPS Works

The NPS process has several steps—from contacting clients to ask for participation to translating the results and implementing procedures to make positive changes. The entire process falls under the following categories:

- Survey client base
- Tabulate results
- Contact promoters and detractors
- Categorize issues based on results of contacts
- Assign issues to be resolved to staff with dates for completion
- Review completion of action plan
- Repeat the process

The first step is to gather a list of the clients you want to contact, and then to send out a letter via e-mail that announces the survey and to encourage them to participate (see Figure 6.1).

Mr. Client
100 Success Street
Anytown, USA 55555

Dear Client:

We want to thank you for your business. Our firm values the relationship we have with you, and we want you to know how much we appreciate you.

Our main goal at the firm is to provide you with services that will help you increase your business and profitability. We want the experience you have with us to be so good that you will actively recommend our firm to your friends and colleagues.

To do this, we need to know how we are doing currently and what we need to do to strengthen our relationship with you so that you never hesitate in recommending us to others.

We will soon send you a short online survey to fill out, which will take you less than 5 minutes to complete. Once we have the results, we would like to schedule a meeting with you to discuss areas where we can improve our services to you.

Again, thanks for your business and we look forward to a long, mutually beneficial relationship.

Sincerely yours,
Amy Vetter
Cherished Advisors, LLC

Figure 6.1 Sample Letter

Mr. Great Client
200 Success Street
Anytown, USA 55555

Dear Client:

Please complete the following survey for Cherished Advisors, LLC:

How likely are you to recommend Cherished Advisors, LLC to your friends and colleagues?
Please answer on a scale of 1 to 10, where 10 is "extremely likely" and 1 is "not likely"? _____

Please explain the reasons for your response to question 1.

_____

_____

_____

_____

If you answered 1 through 8, what are the three most important things Cherished Advisors, LLC
must do to have you answer 9 or 10 in the future?

_____

_____

_____

_____

We appreciate your time and the relationship we have with you,

Cherished Advisors, LLC

Figure 6.2 Survey Letter

Next, you will send out the survey. Figure 6.2 shows is a sample of
what a survey might look like. Note that each survey should be coded
to the client, if possible, so you can link back to the person who worked
on that client.

It is best to send this out by using an online survey tool. The three
keys to successful surveys are how easy it is for you to create the survey
(including templates, design, color, fonts, and background), whether
reporting is available, and how easy it is for your customers or target
audience to take it. Most online tools offer a free trial or basic service
so you can see how it works for you.

Your chosen program should be able to track responses when they
arrive as well as be able to download the data so you can create reports.

For instance, the program should be able to export the e-mail addresses of respondents so you can then reach out to them to convey additional information or alert them to promotions. There are many survey apps available, but here is a look at three that tend to receive high marks:

SurveyMonkey (surveymonkey.com)

One advantage here is that you can customize your surveys with colors, special texts, and even your own logo. You send out your survey through the site's platform or you can create a link that you can send via e-mail or your social media. Also, you can add the survey to your website.

SurveyGizmo (surveygizmo.com)

What is great about this app is that you can add up to five users to the account, so multiple people can access the data, which is ideal if you have a large team. You can also collect surveys offline, and the data will sync with your systems whenever you are connected to the Internet.

Zoho (zoho.com)

You can distribute the survey like SurveyMonkey, and can collect the survey offline like SurveyGizmo. Zoho also offers 50 survey templates from which to choose.

Calculating Your Net Promoter Score

When you receive the survey results, you then need to calculate your NPS. Your clients will be divided into three response categories:

Promoters: 9 or 10

These people are showing that they see value in your company and are more than willing to share their experience with business colleagues and friends. You can learn much from them as they can show you what works that keeps them loyal.

Passives: 7 or 8

These individuals are satisfied, but not necessarily loyal. They like what they receive but make few referrals and when they do they are not enthusiastic. This group can be challenging, since they do like your service, but you need to find what they need to elevate them to promoters.

Detractors: 6 or lower

These people signal the red flags. They are unhappy and feel you don't care about them or their business. However, they offer opportunities to learn about your client services and correct the problem. You often have to probe to find the main area(s) of concern, but often it can help save a client relationship as well as strengthen existing ones. Figure 6.3 shows a breakdown of the NPS numbers.

To determine your NPS, first add up the percent of clients who answered 9 or 10 (meaning "yes, I will recommend you to a friend and I enjoy your service"). You ignore the "passives"—the clients who rate you 7 or 8 on the scale—because this means that you are doing an okay job. And then you *subtract* the percentage of respondents who rated you 1 to 6. For example, say 90 people responded to the survey. Here is how you might calculate the results:

- 50 are promoters (56 percent).
- 20 are passive (ignore).
- 20 are detractors (22 percent).
- Subtract 22 from 56 for a NPS of 34 (56 − 22 = 34).

This calculation is also shown in Figure 6.4.

The higher the score (and closer to 100), the more satisfied are your clients, and the more likely they will be loyal customers who refer your services to people they know. A negative score (or one closer to zero) means you have work to do to strengthen your relationship

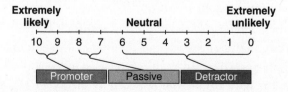

Figure 6.3 NPS Breakdown

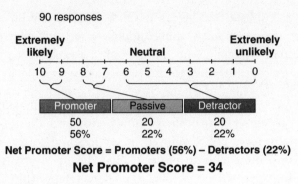

Figure 6.4 Sample NPS Calculation

so they don't provide negative testimonials to potential clients. Both scores offer valuable feedback to help you grow your practice.

Because your surveys are linked to your clients, you know which client said what, and also which team member was responsible for that client. You want to be able to follow up with both the Promoters and the Detractors.

For the Promoters who gave you high scores, you want to discuss what you should keep doing. Learning what is working will ensure that it continues and you can take that knowledge to implement for other clients. For the Detractors, you need to understand why you were given low scores—understand what you are *not* doing well and what you can do to help improve your services.

It is best to gather this follow-up information during your next scheduled meeting to ensure you hear exactly what your client says and feels (which can sometimes be difficult to extract from a written memo or e-mail reply).

You can then bring those results to staff to share and design strategies not only to support what is working but also, and more importantly, to address what needs to be improved. For example, depending on the results, you might identify certain employees who need additional training, change how you present information to the client, or translate your analysis better so the clients can implement it into their business strategies. The results can also be used to recognize and reward team members who are providing excellent customer service, or you can repurpose the feedback as testimonials to use with other clients.

This takes time and effort to implement properly. You want to use the information to your advantage, but not rush to correct without first diagnosing why the client has a problem with an area of your services and what they would suggest you do to improve. You also need to identify whether this is a one-off issue with a single client or it is predominant feedback that you are getting from other clients too.

How can NPS translate into growth? It can occur in two ways: short and long term. Here is an example of how British Gas Services, the United Kingdom's largest gas supplier in the United Kingdom, used NPS to bolster their business. The company was losing money, so they created a NPS process in order to get customer feedback for each installation project, with the goal of gaining real-time insight into how they were doing, so they could make immediate changes.

Over a two-year period, their NPS scores rose from 45 percent to 75 percent. The NPS helped British Gas Services increase revenues by not losing clients, and the company saved money on personnel because they had fewer customer complaints. Overall, their bad debts declined more than 90 percent and profit margins increased to double digits. Best of all, their formerly shrinking revenues surged 30 percent in one year, from 45 percent to 75 percent.[4]

Once you formulate your action plan, communicate it to your client. You might say something like, "Thanks for filling out our survey! We learned what you like about us [mention the specifics and say you will continue to do these things]." Also include a statement such as: "This is what you want us to improve on... [mention the things that came up in the survey as areas you are lacking]. We have committed to improve in the following areas by doing the following things... [as an example: if people said you don't return their calls on a timely basis, you might declare that to be true, and then say, 'We have committed to return calls between the hours of 2 PM and 3 PM every afternoon or within 24 hours of receiving their message in the future.']." Not only are you addressing the issues with your client, but sending a message that you value their input and are working to make your relationship stronger.

You may want to repeat this process every year, if possible—not only to gauge whether you are making improvements where you need them, but also to ensure you are still performing well in the areas where your client receives the most benefit. This way, you can create a baseline and will be able to measure year-over-year growth rate to see exactly where and how your NPS is benefiting your business. No doubt you will see other benefits, too, such as a more engaged staff, as well as happier and more loyal clients who provide more referrals of potential clients.

HOW EMMERMAN, BOYLE & ASSOCIATES, LLC MAINTAINS LASTING CLIENT AND TEAM RELATIONSHIPS

The following interview was conducted by Amy Vetter with David Emmerman, EA and Partner with Emmerman, Boyle & Associates, LLC, Patchogue, New York.

What is your approach to maintaining lasting client relationships? Can you share examples of what you do to keep long-standing clients, as well as an example of when you were at risk for losing a client—what did you do to reaffirm the relationship and why did it work?

Emmerman: We look back to our core thematic goal of customer service. If you provide great customer service by truly appreciating and caring for your client's interests and needs you can establish that lasting relationship. I have many examples of this being true with our clients, as we still have some of my father's original clients from the late 1960s. I can remember back to the relationships that have had rocky points, and often times they were centered around two core issues: communication and expectation. As we have grown, I have noticed that these two fundamental pillars are paramount. Once those two issues are clarified, relationships either are solidified, or it's clear that a change needs to be made, on either side of the engagement.

What do you feel clients are looking for in a long-standing relationship? And how have you changed to help meet that new requirement?

Emmerman: Our clients' needs change along [as] their businesses and lifestyles change. We need to be adaptive and proactive to ensure we stay relevant and connected to our clients. We become critical advisors and confidantes, and it's important to keep that in mind when we meet with them. We have adapted to this by changing how we begin our relationships and ask them for productive feedback that we can share with our team.

What have you learned from a client relationship that eventually fell away that you have applied for ongoing relationships?

Emmerman: Due diligence is important to ensure a client is a good fit as is a clear onboarding process. There is nothing worse than spending a considerable amount of time and effort establishing your value, only to fail at being able to manage the expectations during the onboarding phase. It's easy for a client to lose the perspective on the value you can deliver if you can't get to that work quickly.

Building relationships with your teams is equally important. What special or differentiated compensation programs, benefits, or rewards do you put in place to differentiate your workplace and keep employees happy? How do they work, and why have they been successful?

Emmerman: One thing I have found is that people are not necessarily financially driven, and sometimes appreciation and understanding of what they truly value is just as important. Employees want to feel successful and fulfilled, and that is different for everyone. From a strict compensation model, I prefer to have some type of base salary that can be increased by some type of COLA [cost of living adjustment] based on subjective metrics that are identified in advance. Bonuses should be set around some sort of financial/nonsubjective targets. For example, if the employee is responsible for $100,000 in billings, we want him or her to increase that to $110,000 as a target (targets should be difficult, but attainable), and he or she would get a bonus off of that target. The employee might be able to fully control these metrics, or perhaps other team members are integral to this success, but that only helps the teamwork piece of this.

Identifying great talent is challenging—are there any special interview techniques you have put in place that have been successful in identifying the right candidates for your practice?

Emmerman: I like the idea and principles laid out in *Who: The A Method for Hiring* by Randy Street and Geoff Smart. The most important piece here is to really establish a good and thorough role description and be clear with the interview team as to what they should be interviewing for.

What keeps your employees happy, and how does that affect your client loyalty?

Emmerman: What keeps my employees happy is being valued, appreciated, and feeling successful. If they are matched up with clients whom they love to work with and help to make them feel that way, the loyalty is right there.

Is there any other advice you would offer in terms of building lasting client or employee relationships?

Emmerman: Trust. We went through some organizational help exercises and noticed that trust within a team, or the lack thereof, is a key indicator you have a team that will be successful or needs immediate attention to have a cultural overhaul. Also, it is important that for teams to understand what everyone else does in the organization.

Anything you would change when you look back that you would offer as advice?

Emmerman: I would put the processes in place ahead of running down new business lines and expanding. Culture is important—not only to employees but to management and owners as well. Everyone has to love what they do and where they do it.

LEADERSHIP CAPABILITIES TO GROW THE PEOPLE AROUND YOU: TEAM SATISFACTION AND REWARDS

Keeping customer relationships solid and growing is only part of the equation. Without a committed team in place you run the risk of losing some of your bench strength, which in turn can affect the level of client happiness. Your team should grow along with your clients. A motivated team can better serve your clients and help keep them happy.

As businesses know, replacing employees is a costly and time-consuming endeavor. So your focus should be to recruit the right people for your cherished advisor team and then keep them happy so they want to stay.

In Chapter 2, I showed how the millennial generation are ideal candidates for your team. But how do you keep them around? Employees are motivated to stay with a current job for many reasons, but the main reasons may be surprising. For example, a recent Gallup poll found that 51 percent of workers are not engaged at work.[5] Money is not always a motivator either. Of course, workers want a sufficient salary and other benefits, such as 401(k) plans with generous employee matching, but often a higher salary is not the driving factor for people to leave for another job.

Employees want to be engaged and feel they are part of the business—not just stuck doing their work with no idea of how it impacts the business. Only 40 percent of the average workforce is clearly aware of their company's goals and strategies. The amount of feedback employees receive correlates with their level of engagement. As the leader of your cherished advisor team, you constantly need to make sure your staff knows how critical creating a satisfied client is to the business. Team members often do not see the connection between their roles and the services offered to the client or how their role influences the client's level of satisfaction. Investing in your team is always a way to help identify your next leaders in the office, so as your business grows you have already groomed the right people for their next job.

Implementing a Reward System

Your reward systems should cover four areas: compensation, recognition, appreciation, and benefits. You need to implement all four to increase employee motivation and engagement.

Your first step should be to identify which specific behaviors you want to reward. For example, it could be creating new ideas, improving workflow, and increasing project efficiency. Or the behaviors could be more client-based, such as improving a troublesome relationship or helping a client overcome a specific problem. This way your rewards are set up to complement your business goals.

Extra compensation

Compensation is more than offering an earned raise or bonus. Your team sees the money coming in, so create a way for them to be more connected to the team's overall success with an incentive compensation plan that's directly linked to your team's goals. Changing the makeup of their compensation can help them feel that they are tied to the business's success.

For instance, your NPS can identify areas where you are strongest with your client relationship and correlate those areas to the aspects of your team that support them. You can implement a reward and compensation system for team members to ensure you get the results you want. On the other side, NPS identifies areas for improvement, and you can set up financial rewards for the team and individual members when they accomplish these changes.

Another strategy is something I have used—base salary + commission on net revenue collected. It works like this: After a six-month period, the team gets a percentage of the collected fees that they as a team produced from their clients—net of write-offs and discounts. The advantage here is that it provides a way for team members to make more money when they take on more work, and produce it in a quality way. This provides the incentive to create the behavior you want in the practice and encourages your team to feel more tied to the overall success of the practice.

Recognition

Acknowledge someone's efforts or achievements in front of their peers. You can do this during team meetings or e-mail announcements where you cite specific examples of what the employee has done that has had a positive impact on the organization and its clients.

Appreciation

Appreciation is about expressing personal gratitude, such as through a one-on-one meeting, a handwritten note, or an e-mail message to say, "Thank you—keep up the good work!" It's a small gesture that can go a long way for a team member to feel their work matters.

Benefits

You can offer other benefits that can establish an infrastructure that encourages loyalty from employees—as well as be used as a recruitment tool. For example:

Offer training

Additional training for employees, either in their current roles or for other aspects of the team where they could possibly excel, shows that you value their potential and want to invest in their future growth. Training shouldn't just be for the achievement of continuing education on their technical skills. When you invest in training that helps them in their career, this demonstrates that they can have different and larger roles if they desire, and they won't feel stuck by lack of growth potential and be motivated to look elsewhere.

Change team roles

Even if employees excel in their current positions and are comfortable, offer them the opportunity to participate in other areas. Not only can they broaden their knowledge of the entire business operation, but also it gives other team members help when needed. This technique also reinforces the message that employees don't have to leave the firm to grow their careers.

Create virtual offices

It is easier, now more than ever, for team members to set up virtual offices. There will be times when on-site work is needed, but creating ways for them to work remotely and letting them do so on a regular basis (so they don't have to ask for permission to work away from the office) can help create a positive work environment that your employees will be less likely to want to change and can reinforce their feelings of being trusted and empowered.

Set up flexible schedules

The classic 9-to-5 workday can be antiquated. Virtual offices allow the opportunity for team members to set their own working hours. Again, it's a small way to show you have confidence in team members, and it gives them opportunities to act like their own boss as long as they are delivering quality work, on time and on budget.

Overcoming Fear of Change

Accountants can often find themselves feeling that if something is comfortable and works, then why do anything different? But that approach not only stifles growth for you, your team, and your business, it also gives a false sense of security, because more effort is put toward keeping everything the same instead of making strides to actually protect your business for the future. No industry is immune to change, whether it's related to changing markets, customers, and technology.

Your cherished advisor endeavors are a huge step toward embracing change since you are motivated to break away from the old ways of doing accounting and focusing your energy and resources in a new type of accounting services. But you also will encounter fear of change from another source: your potential clients. Sometimes a customer may rebuff your services, not because they don't value them, but due to the fact that they fear taking on something new. However, you can help your client overcome any hesitation or doubts they may have. Here are some tips to follow.

- *Be honest about the potential risks.* Many people fear what they don't know. Outline the possible risks in details and why they may occur and don't try downplay them. The more your client knows, the more he or she will feel comfortable with the idea of change.

- *Create an all-around consensus.* Change effects the entire operation, so don't just focus on the top people. Enlist everyone in the business who will be influenced by this change to get his or her insight. If change feels like more of a team-effort, it will seems less intimidating.

- *Develop a detailed plan.* Your client will feel much more comfortable with a firm plan in place. Your strategy for implementing change should have a step-by-step process that addresses goals, concerns, potential problems, and a plan to address them when they arise (because they will).

- *Begin small.* A smaller change target like an individual project offers minimal investment and risk for the client, and results that can be easily analyzed. This also offers the opportunity to make adjustments in the process where needed, and can act as a springboard to a larger change initiative.

■ *Measure the results with solid data.* Nothing says progress like facts and figures. Remember numbers don't lie and if your client can see how change is making a difference, they are more likely to embrace it with confidence.

Daily Procedures

Every team's workday can vary depending on the client and project, but as has been shown, communication and regular engagement is key to customer happiness. Keeping track of your communication can avoid any miscommunication or potential issues down the road. Whenever you interact with clients, or just as part of regular team maintenance, make sure the following checkpoints are attended to:

Send recap e-mails

After each meeting, follow up with a detailed e-mail that summarizes the get-together so that each one has a record to revisit when needed. The e-mail also can identify any issues that may have been missed or that need greater attention. The recap e-mail can include any of the following:

■ Date of meeting

■ Issues discussed during meeting

■ Areas accomplished

■ Status of whether timelines are being met

■ Any changes in schedule with the client

■ Schedule next appointment

Add to project tracking template

In Chapter 5, I discussed creating a project plan to monitor progress on an engagement and milestones to track. Update your project plan to reflect any changes from a meeting or other issues that may reflect on timelines or pending deadlines. Even if new changes are needed, create documented services as a scope change on the plan so it's clear to the staff and the client.

Back up all accounting reports and files

Set up a reminder to back up all necessary reports, files, and any other relevant financial information.

Update scheduling

Use any scheduling software or programs you use to review and update all work assignments for your team members. Create a report, or track this in your practice management software, for all weekly meetings or project deadlines. Ensure there are automatic alerts built in so all team members or clients are reminded at least one week in advance.

HOW EISNERAMPER, LLP APPROACHES CLIENT AND TEAM RELATIONSHIPS

The following interview was conducted by Amy Vetter with Michael Lopez, CPA, Partner—Private Business Services Group and Aaron Berson, CPA, Director—Viral Business and Cloud Computing Services of EisnerAmper, LLP in New York City, New York.

What is your approach to maintaining lasting client relationships? Can you share examples of what you do to keep long-standing clients as well as an example of when you were at risk for losing a client—what did you do to reaffirm the relationship, and why did it work?

Lopez and Berson: We focus on what keeps clients up at night. We hear their pain points and find a way either internally or externally to make our clients' lives better. In building a lasting relationship, we make sure we are not afraid of losing a client. To keep long-standing clients, we build a relationship that goes beyond our work. For example, one construction client began with us helping with a stressful business situation. Since then, we speak periodically about their lives and their families. When the client's father passed, we sent food for a night of mourning with our condolences. We have sent celebratory packages for large life events. Additionally, we listen to their pain and joy, and we make genuine efforts to help any way we can.

Another client had just gone through a period of having an internal employee steal from them. Management had turned over all financial responsibilities to an employee, and thus our interactions with the owners were limited. When this fraud was discovered, our relationship had been questioned, since this individual had hired us. To reaffirm the client, we had an in-person meeting, changed our engagement team, and again listened to their fears and did what we could to help. Here, we had to focus on our trustworthiness, as the client was obviously having trust issues. We have worked through this and now do the outsourced back office for the client, which we did not do previously.

What are the greatest obstacles you have encountered for building lasting client relationships and why? What did you do to overcome?

Lopez and Berson: Creating a sense of importance for each customer is a significant obstacle to building lasting customer relationships. As our firm works with small businesses, this is a consistent challenge. Inevitably, there is a point where our clients question whether they are too small for such a large firm. Often this comes up during our initial talks with a prospect, when the relationship is new. To overcome this, we assure them we love working with small businesses because so many care about their business more than larger corporations since they are building it and not working for it. The next step is to have a conversation around their needs, and spending time to hear their pain and demonstrate the advantages of working with us.

To further create this feeling of importance, we continue to be involved in the relationship, whether or not we are doing the work or staff is involved. This often means having phone calls, video chats, or personal visits from time to time, and not only around our work. When we only interact around work, we are viewed only in that manner and not as someone committed to them.

What do you feel clients are looking for in a long-standing relationship? How have you changed to help meet that new requirement?

Lopez and Berson: Clients are looking for a one-stop shop. They want an advisor, not an accountant. In the past, we have been amazingly technical and knowledgeable with our clients. However, they want or need more. Often businesses don't have advisors, or those who know their businesses as we do. To assist with this, we have built our Virtual Business Services group—this is a CAS [client accounting services]-type group. We act as a CFO/controller or full back office to the client. Thus, we facilitate almost everything at times, and are involved in business discussions from pricing of products or services to interfacing with money sources and everything in between.

Building relationships with your teams is equally important. What special or differentiated compensation programs, benefits, or rewards do you put in place to differentiate your workplace and keep employees happy? How do they work, and why have they been successful?

Lopez and Berson: For compensation, we offer a bonus correlated to any new business brought in by a nonpartner. To differentiate our work environment, we take pride and put great effort into fostering ownership, advancement, and growth. We allow staff to own our client relationships. To do this, we involve as many as possible in the pitch process and early stage of the client work. This allows us to teach our young professionals the skills of managing clients. We encourage our staff to find a niche they like and provide training and support to make them an expert. Additionally, we allow working from home or remotely when possible to align with a staff person's life and evolving needs. We also understand our staff have great ideas, so we have ways to allow for innovation and to allow an open dialog to explore what is important to our staff's day-to-day work.

Identifying great talent is challenging. Are there any special interview techniques you have put in place that have been successful in identifying the right candidates for your practice?

Lopez and Berson: We make sure new members are a good cultural fit and are driven. We want our office to feel entrepreneurial and energetic, so we have identified traits that contribute to this type of environment. This list lets us know what we are looking for in a defined way, and we can direct the interview process to uncover whether these traits are present.

How have you identified successors for leadership roles in your practice? Do you let them know? Do you have mentorship programs? What skills do you look for in potential leaders to mentor?

Lopez and Berson: We are always looking for successors for leadership roles. That should be a major focal point in growing any professional service practice. Most important is for the candidate to be able to communicate well. They should be able to think out of the box and have strong visionary skills. Of course, they need to be grounded in the technical aspect of the business, but often we find that technical skills alone don't cut it. And we do have mentorship programs to continue to discuss these types of issues with the express purpose of bringing those communication skills to the forefront.

What keeps your employees happy, and how does that affect your client loyalty?

Lopez and Berson: Our flexible work environment, the opportunity for ownership of clients, the opportunity for promotions based on performance, and an entrepreneurial mind-set. These factors contribute to a happier and more committed workforce. In turn, this creates a better experience for our clients, which leads to them viewing us as a true trusted advisor.

Is there any other advice you would offer in terms of building lasting client or employee relationships?

Lopez and Berson: Listen to your employees. Find a way to enable a frank and open line of communication where if an employee feels something, negative or positive, they can communicate it and be heard. There is nothing worse than working at a firm that claims to listen to its employees, yet every time an issue is raised, nothing is done. This doesn't mean you have to make every suggested change, but have a discussion about why the employee suggests this change is important. Sometimes there is an underlying issue that can be addressed.

SUCCESSION PLANNING TACTICS FOR BRINGING UP THE NEXT GENERATION OF LEADERSHIP

A great cherished advisor team is only as strong as its members, which is why recruiting the right talent is so important. Many start-ups, looking to save money, might opt to hire subcontractors to build their team, which has definite advantages, such as not having to pay payroll taxes, only paying for chargeable hours, and being able to eliminate the position as needed with no payout. However, your cherished advisor practice is about building personal relationships with clients, and it is tough to do this with staff members who are not really part of your team or invested in its success. Plus, there is a lack of control in their schedules and availability, and there is even a chance they could directly or indirectly compete with your business. Here are some tips:

- *Hire full-time employees.* Hiring full-time employees establishes more loyalty, allowing you to build the stability and foundation that are key to gaining a client's trust and keeping him or her satisfied. Of course, there are more costs related to employees in terms of paying for actual work performance, payroll taxes, and other company benefits like health insurance and paid vacations. But the benefits for this type of investment outweigh any short-term cost savings you may have with subcontractors.

- *Find talent online.* Nowadays, there are many outlets available to find the right kind of workers for your team—for instance, recruiting websites like LinkedIn, Monster, Craigslist, and CareerBuilder. You should ensure your website is set up to advertise openings for people to send in resumes. Once you implement the marketing tactics I discussed in Chapter 4, your website will portray your vision, mission, and services. This will help potential recruits to understand whether they share your company's values.

- *Utilize your social network platform.* Social networks can be a great tool, as you can speak directly to many millennials, whom you want to attract.

Your own networking can be helpful too. Here are some suggestions:

- *Develop relationships with job placement and recruiting organizations.* Work with local and state university placement offices and professional recruiters.

- *Attend industry professional associations and conferences.* Utilize team members to frequent industry professional associations and conferences and keep their eyes open for potential candidates. Involve them in the hiring process, too. Their insight can offer various perspectives and help you make a more thorough hire.

- *Advertise.* Place ads on professional association websites and magazines.

- *Reach out to your colleagues.* Have they recently passed on any candidates that they liked but would possibly be a better fit for the role you have open?

Creating Internal Processes

To improve and maintain your NPS, and thus have clients who are happy and satisfied, you need to have the right internal processes to maintain client happiness. You should develop internal processes, from hiring team members to employee trainings and reviews to managing daily procedures and overseeing administrative tasks.

Hiring Staff and the Interview Process

I previously discussed the advantages of recruiting millennials for your cherished advisor team, as they provide the desire, and in many ways, a vast area of interest and expertise that is valuable to your team's services. But how do you go from recruiting to hiring essential team members? During the initial interviewing phase, look for key personality traits. Sometimes this is not always easy to judge in brief encounters, but looking for signs of these traits can better help you identify potential key hires. They also can help team members grow in their initial hiring position, as well as help you identify people for larger roles on the team. For example:

Interpersonal Skills

This includes verbal communication; nonverbal communication, which is how a person expresses him or herself without words and body language; and listening skills (how they interpret what you say during the interview).

Professionalism

How people conduct themselves in a professional setting often can speak volumes about how they will approach client relations. This includes everything from appearance to mannerisms to small details like showing up on time and being prepared.

Technical Skills

What skills does the person need to possess? If they don't have these skills, can they acquire them in the position? Sometimes, it is easier to hire someone who has many of the needed skills and provide further training than to wait for the so-called perfect candidate.

Willingness to Learn

This ties into the technical skills part, but the ideal team member also has a desire to learn new aspects of their job and the industry as a whole. If he or she is content doing one job, the same way, indefinitely, it is doubtful that person will be a valuable asset as your business grows.

Willingness to Travel to Clients

Depending on the team member's role, their interaction with clients may be limited or more in-depth. It is best to know up front how willing they are to interact with clients and to what degree.

Pay Scale

This can always be a tricky part of negotiation. You will have a budget in mind that you want to stick with, but make sure your pay scale matches what you want from the team member. You should take into consideration the level of technical expertise and skill sets needed. Paying more for the skills you need now and in the future will go a long way toward avoiding the revolving door of employees. Remember, it is always cheaper to pay more for team members who will stay longer than to pay less for a short-term worker.

Employee Onboarding and Reviews

To ensure a smooth transition from the hire, you should put in place an initial checklist to cover the support you and your new team member need for success. These checkpoints can help you gauge the employee's progress and make sure that he or she is meeting your expectations and company goals. Here are a few key items that should be included in your new-hire checklist:

Employee Contracts

Has all the necessary paperwork been filled out and placed on file? Be sure to work with an attorney in your area to ensure you have the right legal protections. This can include items such as the offer letter/employment agreement and a non-compete agreement that covers areas such as confidentiality, nonsolicitation, and noncompetition.

Shadowing

Shadowing is monitoring a co-worker on the job to gain greater insight and knowledge into that person's particular work and responsibilities. Shadowing can have two specific advantages. For a new hire, shadowing someone in a similar job can allow exposure to that environment and the opportunity to learn and ask questions without being overwhelmed or on the line to get the work done. It can also be used as a tool for seasoned workers who may want to explore new opportunities before making a full commitment.

90-Day Review After Hire Date

This review is often used as a benchmark to provide feedback to the employee that gauges how he or she is fitting in and whether short-term goals are being met. While this is not always the best time-frame to gather all the information you and your new hire needs, it's a good point to highlight early successes and identify potential problems before they grow. Make this get-together informal and conversational. It should be a learning process for both parties and a chance to measure what is working and what needs help.

Staff Engagement Evaluations

The earlier referenced Gallup poll also reported that only 30 percent of workers are engaged in their jobs. It is essential that you keep communication open with your team members in order to create enthusiasm and dedication to the practice. If they don't feel engaged or challenged, they not only will begin to underperform, but will be more likely to look elsewhere for more stimulating work.

A common approach for many businesses is to create a yearly survey that employees fill out to help measure their personal level of engagement. While this can be helpful, it does have flaws. For instance, it tends to highlight engagement based on recent events over a short period—not a longer time frame. Also, you sometimes have to take the results with a grain of salt, as employees may tell you what you want to hear rather than how they really feel.

There are other, more direct measures to help companies better understand team member engagement levels. Here are some examples from Ryan Fuller of the *Harvard Business Review* on how a company might better evaluate staff.[6]

- *The amount of work that occurs outside of normal working hours (e.g., evenings and weekends).* This is a good indicator of discretionary effort.

- *The number of network connections and time spent with people outside of immediate team or region.* Building of broad networks beyond core team is a sign of high engagement.

- *Time spent collaborating directly with customers outside of normal scope of work.* This and other measures like it can indicate people are highly engaged enough to help their colleagues even though they might not get credit for it.

There are other metrics you can employ to better understand what engages team members and how you might implement them. Here are some more examples from Fuller:

- *Time spent in one-on-ones with their manager per week.* Engagement typically increases as an individual gets more time with his or her boss.

- *Time spent in presence of skip-level leadership.* Engagement can increase as people get more exposure to colleagues up the ladder.

- *Network quality and breadth of their manager.* Engagement often increases in people who have well-connected direct managers.

- *The percent of a manager's time spent with team.* A number that's too low or too high typically decreases engagement.

Interim/Year-End Evaluations

Some companies employ in-between and year-end evaluations, or some combination. The annual evaluation is more common, but often it's seen as a necessary chore rather that a tool that can further gauge progress for your team members on the business. The key to effective evaluations is not to make it about criticism or judgment, but rather a process to explore what is working, why, and how to build from that. You want to give feedback in real time, not wait for the end of the year and have it be a surprise that the team member is not performing at the level you want. When you approach your evaluations, you should take the following into consideration to ensure you and the team member receive the information you both need.

Prepare

What are the main areas you want to cover and key messages you want to convey? What do you want the team member to think about at the end? Put time and effort into what you want the outcome to be. Get further insight from the person's co-workers, managers, or supervisors.

Set Clear Objectives

Set up the evaluation's objectives and share with the team member, and give them the opportunity to add anything they would like to talk about.

Be Candid About Problems—and Generous When Praise Is Due

Let the employee know how much he or she is valued, but make sure the praise has measurable specifics. For example, what did he or she do that was good, and why? Often employees don't see how their efforts affect the business's success, and this is an opportunity for them to see how they help the company, and thus better understand their value. Take the same approach when talking about areas of improvement. Don't dwell on what he or she did that was not good. Instead, show how improvements in these areas can help the business as well as their co-workers.

Make it a Dialogue

Ultimately, this is about you receiving feedback from the employee. Let him or her tell you what works or doesn't and what could be improved. No doubt, you will learn something of value, too.

Schedule a Future Talk

After the evaluation, outline a detailed strategy with specific objectives for improvement if needed. Also, arrange another review not too far in the future for a follow-up conversation, like a few months. This can help gauge what progress has been made and whether there should be any changes to the strategy.

Further Resources to Develop Your Business

General Dwight Eisenhower once said, "plans are nothing, but planning is everything." Instant results cannot be expected—they take time. In Chapter 2, I explained the importance of doing a SWOT (strengths, weaknesses, opportunities, and threats) analysis to help identify potential vertical industry niche markets. Once your cherished advisor practice begins, you should randomly complete a SWOT analysis for your company as a check-in on how you are doing and where there are opportunities to improve or acquire.

Whatever your SWOT analysis shows as areas you need to address, you have to put a plan together to implement the right strategy in order for it to succeed. This is where SMART (specific, measureable, achievable, realistic, and time-bound) goals come into play. They can help you execute any type of goal you have for your business. With all of the concepts that are presented in this book, now is the time to figure out where to start. SMART goals can help you organize your ideas and ensure you don't set yourself up for failure by taking on more than you can handle. It's important to set goals that are realistic so that you can feel a sense of accomplishment as you move through this transformation journey.

The thinking behind SMART is that if your business goal is well defined and there are many tools in place to measure and track its progress, it will be easier to achieve the goal. SMART breaks down like this:

Specific. What is specific about the goal?

Measurable. Are there outcomes where the goal can be measured?

Achievable. Is the goal achievable? If not, what needs to change to make it so?

Realistic. Is the goal realistic to meet performance expectations or professional development?

Time-bound. When will this goal be accomplished? How will you know?

SMART goals keep you from tackling goals that are too broad or not well defined, which can make achieving them difficult if not impossible. Say your goal is to increase revenue by $220,000 within the next year. Your SMART would break down like this:

> Increase revenue by $220,000 within 12 months. Goal No. 1: Identify one to two vertical industry markets to approach, which project leader will be assigned, and what they will do by March 31. The two team tactics to achieve that goal will be to first review a current client list for potentials, which another team member will deliver by December 31, and then arrange a staff meeting to generate other ideas and possible leads, which another team member will arrange and conduct by December 31.

In this example, the objective and outcome are clear, and there are two strategies to find potential clients in place with go-to people in charge and specific time frames to complete. All of the elements of a SMART goal are in place. You can see how easily the goal could fall away if one of the parts is missing.

You can use SMART goals to accomplish any goal your team has—whether in the beginning, when you are working to land clients, to outlining short- and long-term objectives to implement strategies based on your NPS to improve client relationships. This will help you to narrow down what to focus on during a certain time period in order to create the long-lasting client relationships you desire.

SUMMARY

Securing long-term client–accountant relationships is the ultimate goal to help build and grow your cherished advisor business. When you have established yourself as a cherished advisor with a client, the additional rewards you can reap from the relationship can appear in different ways. When you have shown your clients how you can help them—and in return, they begin to see the results in their business—they are more inclined to reach out to you for other services.

This is the kind of trusted relationship you want to develop. However, as with any type of relationship, it takes work and commitment to make it last. By applying specific client support tools and measuring client happiness, you can identify and address potential issues before they become problematic. The ultimate goal is for you to be a central point of contact for your client so that you hear about the things they want to do in their business first and ensure they work with people you trust as advisors and experts as well.

Keeping customer relationships solid and growing is only part of the equation. Without a committed team in place, you run the risk of losing some of your bench strength, which in turn can affect the level of client happiness. Your team should grow along with your clients since a motivated and satisfied team will be less likely to leave for other positions and thus can better serve your clients and help keep them happy.

ENDNOTES

1. Brian Solis, *X: The Experience When Business Meets Design* (Hoboken, NJ: Wiley, 2015), www.xthebook.com.
2. "The Capability Gap 2015: Are You Developing the Skills Employers Are Looking For?" Hays plc, accessed June 22, 2017, www.hays.co.uk/capability-gap-2015/index.htm.
3. Jennifer Kaplan, "The Inventor of Customer Satisfaction Surveys Is Sick of Them, Too," May 2016, *Bloomberg.com*, retrieved June 5, 2016, https://blog.chartmogul.com/net-promoter-score/.
4. "Good Profits and Growth: How Net Promoter Helps Companies Thrive in a Customer-Driven World." The European Business Review, accessed August 07, 2017, http://www.europeanbusinessreview.com/good-profits-and-growth-how-net-promoter-helps-companies-thrive-in-a-customer-driven-world/.
5. Amy Adkins, "Majority of U.S. Employees Not Engaged Despite Gains in 2014," January 28, 2015, Gallup.com, accessed May 26, 2017, www.gallup.com/poll/181289/majority-employees-not-engaged-despite-gains-2014.aspx.
6. Ryan Fuller, "A Primer on Measuring Employee Engagement," November 17, 2014, *Harvard Business Review*, accessed May 26, 2017, https://hbr.org/2014/11/a-primer-on-measuring-employee-engagement.

About the Author

Amy Vetter is an accomplished business executive, serial entrepreneur, national speaker, CPA, CITP, and CGMA. She has held a variety of corporate executive positions and leadership roles overseeing customer programs, sales, education, and marketing functions, both nationally and internationally, such as being the chief relationship officer (CRO)—Partner Channel for Xero Americas. Prior to Xero, she was the CPA programs leader for Intacct Corporation and performed many roles in the accountant professional division with Intuit, Inc. Additionally, she has experience running multiple client accounting services practices, including her own companies and as a partner in a CPA firm.

Amy is an advocate and evangelist for entrepreneurship and the accounting profession. She has inspired thousands of business owners, corporate leaders, and accounting professionals as a keynote speaker. Amy regularly speaks on business, financial, technology, and work-life harmony topics at hundreds of conferences and universities throughout the United States and internationally.

Along with her corporate life, Amy is a third-generation woman entrepreneur with diverse experiences, including owning and operating her own accounting practice, yoga studios, and other business ventures. She is currently the owner and founder of DRISHTIQ yoga, a studio that offers more than 50 classes per week in addition to virtual yoga and teacher training programs.

Amy has been recognized as one of the Top 100 Most Influential People in Accounting three years in a row by *Accounting Today* and was named one of the Most Powerful Women in Accounting by *CPA Practice Advisor*. She has also been nominated as a Woman to Watch by the California Certified Public Accountant (CALCPA) State Society, and was selected by *CPA Technology Advisor* as an outstanding 40 under 40 technology-based accountant in 2006 and 2009.

Amy is an active member of a variety of professional accounting associations, including:

- The American Institute of Certified Public Accountants (AICPA) Information Management Technology Assurance (IMTA) Executive Committee;
- An AICPA CITP Champion;
- A CALCPA MAP State Committee member;
- A CALCPA Women's Leadership Forum Conference Committee member; and,
- An Ohio State Certified Public Accountants (OSCPA)— Cincinnati's Women's Initiative Committee member.

Amy regularly contributes her life-lessons and best practices on entrepreneurship, technology, and the accounting industry to *Inc.com*, *Entrepreneur.com*, *Fast Company*, *The Business Journals*, *CPA Practice Advisor*, *Accounting WEB*, and *Accounting Today*. She is also the author of the book *Business, Balance, & Bliss: How the B³ Method Can Transform Your Career and Life*.

Amy lives with her husband and two sons in Ohio. Learn more about Amy on her website at www.amyvetter.com, and follow her on LinkedIn, Twitter, Facebook, or Instagram via @amyvettercpa.

Index